OECD Compendium of Productivity Indicators 2015

This work is published under the responsibility of the Secretary-General of the OECD. The opinions expressed and arguments employed herein do not necessarily reflect the official views of OECD member countries.

This document and any map included herein are without prejudice to the status of or sovereignty over any territory, to the delimitation of international frontiers and boundaries and to the name of any territory, city or area.

Please cite this publication as:
OECD (2015), *OECD Compendium of Productivity Indicators 2015*, OECD Publishing, Paris.
http://dx.doi.org/10.1787/pdtvy-2015-en

ISBN 978-92-64-22953-2 (print)
ISBN 978-92-64-22957-0 (PDF)

Series: OECD Compendium of Productivity Indicators
ISSN 2225-2118 (print)
ISSN 2225-2126 (online)

The statistical data for Israel are supplied by and under the responsibility of the relevant Israeli authorities. The use of such data by the OECD is without prejudice to the status of the Golan Heights, East Jerusalem and Israeli settlements in the West Bank under the terms of international law.

Photo credits: Cover © Shutterstock/AnatolyM.

Corrigenda to OECD publications may be found on line at: *www.oecd.org/about/publishing/corrigenda.htm*.

Foreword

Productivity measures how efficiently production inputs, such as labour and capital, are being used in an economy to produce a given level of output. It is considered a key source of economic growth and competitiveness and, as such, internationally comparable indicators of productivity are central for assessing economic performance.

The OECD Compendium of Productivity Indicators *presents a broad overview of recent and longer term trends in productivity levels and growth in OECD countries. It highlights the key measurement issues faced when compiling cross-country comparable productivity indicators and describes the caveats needed in analyses. It examines the role of productivity as the main driver of economic growth and convergence, and the contributions of labour, capital and MFP in driving economic growth. It looks at the contribution of individual industries or sectors. It explores the link between productivity, trade and international competitiveness. And it analyses the trend as compared to the cyclical patterns of labour and multifactor productivity growth.*

The 2015 OECD Compendium of Productivity Indicators *has been prepared by Frédéric Parrot and Maria Belen Zinni (Statistics Directorate), with contributions from Agnès Cimper (Directorate for Science, Technology and Innovation). The work benefitted from guidance and comments by Nadim Ahmad and Mariarosa Lunati (Statistics Directorate) and Colin Webb (Directorate for Science, Technology and Innovation). Particular thanks go to Gyorgy Gyomai (Statistics Directorate) for helpful comments and fruitful discussions on trend estimations.*

Table of contents

Figures

Follow OECD Publications on:

 *http://twitter.com/OECD_Pubs*

 *http://www.facebook.com/OECDPublications*

 *http://www.linkedin.com/groups/OECD-Publications-4645871*

 *http://www.youtube.com/oecdilibrary*

 *http://www.oecd.org/oecddirect/*

This book has...

Look for the *StatLinks* at the bottom of the tables or graphs in this book. To download the matching Excel® spreadsheet, just type the link into your Internet browser, starting with the *http://dx.doi.org* prefix, or click on the link from the e-book edition.

Executive summary

GDP growth in the OECD area is beginning to gradually strengthen, years after the start of the global financial crisis. Nevertheless, the pace has varied across countries and a sustainable recovery does not appear to have yet been established, with several OECD countries facing the challenge of slower trend growth. A good understanding of the role and the drivers of productivity growth is thus crucial to strengthening the recovery and improving growth and living standards in the longer term. The *OECD Compendium of Productivity Indicators* provides the ingredients for this by examining both longer term trends of productivity and how the crisis has affected patterns of productivity growth and its components across countries.

Key findings

Longer term productivity trends

- Productivity growth is key to improving GDP per capita and hence living standards. In the last fifteen years, differences in GDP per capita growth across OECD countries can be mainly attributed to differences in growth in GDP per hour worked (labour productivity). In contrast, labour utilisation (hours worked per capita) has hardly changed.
- Very high growth rates in GDP per capita have meant that some countries with initially low GDP per capita levels have converged towards average income levels in the OECD. This process of convergence has typically been driven by strong growth in labour productivity growth. Nonetheless, differences in per capita incomes across OECD countries remained significant in 2013 mainly owing to differences in labour productivity levels and marginally to labour utilisation.
- Between 1995 and 2013, most of the growth in labour productivity reflected growth in multifactor productivity (MFP) and capital input. However, the empirical evidence confirms the pro-cyclical pattern of MFP, which follows GDP growth very closely, not only in terms of the direction but also its magnitude.
- Productivity growth in the non-agricultural business sector was almost entirely driven by manufacturing and business sector services. In general, the manufacturing sector continues to have higher productivity growth than business sector services, while the strong contribution of services reflect a continuing shift in employment and value added towards specialised services.
- Labour productivity growth varies substantially across business sector services. Those services more exposed to international competition and which typically use modern, information and telecommunication (ICT) technologies generally had much higher, and more volatile, productivity growth between 1995 and 2013.
- During the last ten years, the G7 and most of the early members of the euro area have increased their competitiveness, as measured by unit labour costs (ULC). Very low increases in ULCs have typically been achieved by keeping unit labour costs low in both, manufacturing and business sector services. Moreover, countries with relatively low growth in ULC also displayed strong growth in labour productivity.

- Low labour costs have been an important driver of export performance for Germany. The results for G7 countries suggest that global market shares have decreased over the last 15 years.
- Since the mid-1980s, trends in labour productivity growth have varied across G7 countries. Interestingly, indicators suggest that trend labour productivity typically declined since the mid-1990s or early 2000s in G7 countries.

Impact of the crisis on productivity

- After the 2008 financial crisis, labour productivity growth has fallen significantly in most OECD countries and this decline is broadly spread across sectors. However, in a few countries, labour productivity growth seems to have picked up recently, albeit sometimes coupled with declines in output.
- Similarly, there was a sharp fall in MFP in some countries, and there are risks that this could herald declining longer term trends in labour productivity growth.
- Within the euro area, some countries recorded strong falls in ULCs. However, this does not necessarily imply improved relative competiveness as the falls often went hand in hand with significant falls in output and labour inputs.
- Indeed, labour input fell in many countries, sometimes through reducing average hours worked per person engaged but also through job cuts. During such periods, head-counts are even less reliable as a possible proxy for measuring hours worked than during more stable times.

Reader's guide

Productivity is commonly defined as a ratio between the volume of output and the volume of inputs. In other words, it measures how efficiently production inputs, such as labour and capital, are being used in an economy to produce a given level of output. Productivity is considered a key source of economic growth and competitiveness and, as such, internationally comparable indicators of productivity are central for assessing economic performance.

This *OECD Compendium of Productivity Indicators* presents a broad overview of recent and longer term trends in productivity in OECD countries, providing insights on:

- The role played by labour, capital and multifactor productivity growth in driving economic growth.
- The contribution of individual industries or sectors to aggregate labour productivity growth.
- The link between productivity and international competitiveness.

Measures of productivity

There are different measures of productivity. The key distinguishing factor reflects the policy focus but data availability can also play an important role.

Labour productivity, measured as Gross Domestic Product (GDP) per hour worked, is one of the most widely used measures of productivity. Productivity based on hours worked better captures the use of labour inputs than productivity based on numbers of persons employed. Generally, the source for total hours worked is the *OECD National Accounts Statistics* (database), although other sources are necessarily used where data are lacking. Work continues at the national level to develop the necessary source data but despite the progress and ongoing efforts, for some countries, the measurement of hours worked still suffers from a number of statistical problems that can hinder international comparability.

To take account of the role of **capital inputs** in the production process, the preferred measure is the flow of productive services that can be drawn from the cumulative stock of past investments (such as machinery and equipment). These services are estimated by the OECD using the rate of change of the productive capital stock, which takes into account wear and tear, retirements and other sources of reduction in the productive capacity of fixed capital assets. The price of capital services per asset is measured as their rental price. In principle, the latter could be directly observed if markets existed for all capital services. In practice, however, rental prices have to be imputed for most assets, using the implicit rent that capital goods' owners "pay" to themselves (the user costs of capital).

The statistical data for Israel are supplied by and under the responsibility of the relevant Israeli authorities or third parties. The use of such data by the OECD is without prejudice to the status of the Golan Heights, East Jerusalem and Israeli settlements in the West Bank under the terms of international law.

After computing the contributions of labour and capital to output, so-called ***multifactor productivity (MFP)*** can be derived. It measures, therefore, the residual growth that cannot be explained by changes in labour and capital inputs. MFP is often perceived as a pure measure of technological change, but, in practice, it should be interpreted in a broader sense that partly reflects the way capital and labour inputs are measured. Changes in MFP reflect the effects of changes in management practices, brand names, organisational change, general knowledge, network effects, spillovers from production factors, adjustment costs, economies of scale, the effects of imperfect competition and measurement errors.

Gains in productivity also influence the development of unit labour costs (ULCs), one of the most commonly used indicators to assess a country's international competitiveness. However, the ability of ULCs to inform policies targeting international competitiveness may be limited. This relates to the increasing need to take into account growing international fragmentation of production, the effects of which on competitiveness may not be captured sufficiently by ULCs.

The OECD *Productivity Statistics* (database)

Since its launch in 2004, the *OECD Productivity Statistics* (database) (PDB) has provided annual estimates of labour and multifactor productivity growth (MFP) as a tool to analyse the drivers of economic growth in OECD member countries. The database includes the following indicators:

- Labour productivity levels
- Growth in labour productivity
- Capital input measures
- Labour and capital cost shares
- Multifactor productivity
- Unit labour costs.

Annex A presents the definition of each indicator and the computation method.

Country, time and industry coverage

Countries have recently started to update their national accounts data on the basis of the *System of National Accounts 2008*, which recognised, amongst other changes, that expenditures on research and development be treated as investment (see Annex D). The pace of meeting the new standard varies across countries, meaning that some care is needed in comparing across countries. For all OECD countries except Chile, Japan, Norway and Turkey, the indicators presented are based on the 2008 SNA. For Portugal, growth accounts are presented on a 1993 SNA basis, whereas the labour productivity and unit labour cost indicators are presented on a 2008 SNA basis. For New Zealand, growth accounts are presented on a 2008 SNA basis, whereas the labour productivity and unit labour cost indicators are presented on a 1993 SNA basis.

Major revisions in international standards always provide countries an opportunity to introduce quality improvements to their national accounts, by including newly developed and/or enhanced data sources and by improving their methodologies more generally.

This publication looks at longer term trends in productivity growth and its components, but also how the 2008 financial and the euro area crises affected patterns within and across countries. To this end, indicators are typically presented for three distinctive time periods: 1995-2013; 2001-07; and 2007-13. For each country, the average value in the three different periods only takes into account the years for which data are available for the respective indicator and its components.

The OECD *Compendium of Productivity Indicators* includes data for 34 OECD member countries depending on data availability. The figures in this publication use ISO codes for country names:

AUS	Australia	HUN	Hungary	POL	Poland
AUT	Austria	IRL	Ireland	PRT	Portugal
BEL	Belgium	ISL	Iceland	SVK	Slovak Republic
CAN	Canada	ISR	Israel	SVN	Slovenia
CHL	Chile	ITA	Italy	ESP	Spain
CZE	Czech Republic	JPN	Japan	SWE	Sweden
DNK	Denmark	KOR	Korea	CHE	Switzerland
EST	Estonia	LUX	Luxembourg	TUR	Turkey
FIN	Finland	MEX	Mexico	GBR	United Kingdom
FRA	France	NLD	Netherlands	USA	United States
DEU	Germany	NOR	Norway		
GRC	Greece	NZL	New Zealand		

Throughout this publication, the sectoral breakdown follows the International Standard Industry Classification of all Economic Activities (ISIC). Countries are presented if data are available according to its latest version, ISIC Rev. 4, or the European equivalent NACE Rev. 2 (*Nomenclature statistique des activités économiques dans la Communauté européenne*).

Data are provided for the total economy and for individual sectors in the "non-agricultural business sector, excluding real estate" (ISIC Rev. 4 Codes B-N, excl. L). These include: B – Mining and quarrying; C – Manufacturing; D – Electricity, gas, steam and air conditioning supply; E – Water supply; sewerage, waste management and remediation activities; F – Construction; as well as G-N excluding L – Business sector services, excluding real estate.

Business sector services (ISIC Rev. 4 Codes G-N, excl. L) include: G – Wholesale and retail trade; repair of motor vehicles and motorcycles; H – Transportation and storage; I – Accommodation and food service activities; J – Information and communication; K – Financial and insurance activities; M – Professional, scientific and technical activities; N – Administrative and support service activities. Real estate activities (ISIC Rev. 4 Code L) are excluded, as their value-added includes the imputation made for the dwelling services provided and consumed by home-owners.

The business sector also excludes activities that are often provided by non market producers. This reflects the fact that non-market activities are measured on a sum-of-costs approach in current prices, with an implicit imputation made for labour productivity growth (usually zero) for volume estimates, together with an assumption of zero net operating surplus. These activities comprise: O – Public administration and defence; compulsory social security; P – Education; Q – Human health and social work activities; R – Arts, entertainment and recreation; S – Other service activities; T – Activities of households as employers; undifferentiated goods- and services-producing activities of households for own use; U – Activities of extraterritorial organisations and bodies.

Chapter 1

Economic growth and productivity

Size of GDP

Gross Domestic Product (GDP) is the standard measure of the value of final goods and services produced by a country during a period minus the value of imports. GDP per capita is a core indicator of economic performance and commonly used as a broad measure of average living standards or economic well-being.

Key facts

In 2013, the size of GDP for the OECD as a whole was about USD 47 700 billion based on current PPPs. In the same year, GDP per capita for the OECD area was USD 37 848. Four countries recorded GDP per capita in excess of USD 50 000 in 2013 – Luxembourg, Norway, Switzerland, and the United States while in 18 countries, GDP per capita was below the OECD average. GDP per capita for Turkey and Mexico was less than half the level of the OECD total.

Since the outset of the financial crisis in 2007, GDP growth has slowed in all OECD countries compared with the 2001-07 period.

Definition

Countries calculate GDP in their own currencies. In order to compare across countries these estimates have to be converted into a common currency. Often the conversion is made using current exchange rates but these can give a misleading comparison of the true volumes of final goods and services in GDP. A better approach is to use purchasing power parities (PPPs). PPPs are currency converters that control for differences in the price levels of products between countries and so allow an international comparison of the volumes of GDP and of the size of economies.

Information on data for Israel: *http://dx.doi.org/10.1787/888932315602*.

Comparability

The measure of GDP is overall comparable across countries, although not all countries have yet implemented the latest international standard (the 2008 SNA) which can impact on comparisons of GDP. The measurement of the non-observed economy can also affect comparability, but for OECD economies, in general, this is not thought to be significant.

Population estimates are comparable across countries. However, some care is needed in interpretation: for example Luxembourg and, to a lesser extent, Switzerland have a relatively large number of frontier workers. Such workers contribute to GDP but are excluded from the population figures, which is one of the reasons why cross-country comparisons of income per capita based on gross or net national income are also relevant.

Sources and further reading

OECD National Accounts Statistics (database), *http://dx.doi.org/10.1787/na-data-en*.

Figure 1.1. **Gross domestic product, current PPPs and current exchange rates**

The seven largest economies in the OECD, percentage of OECD total, 2013

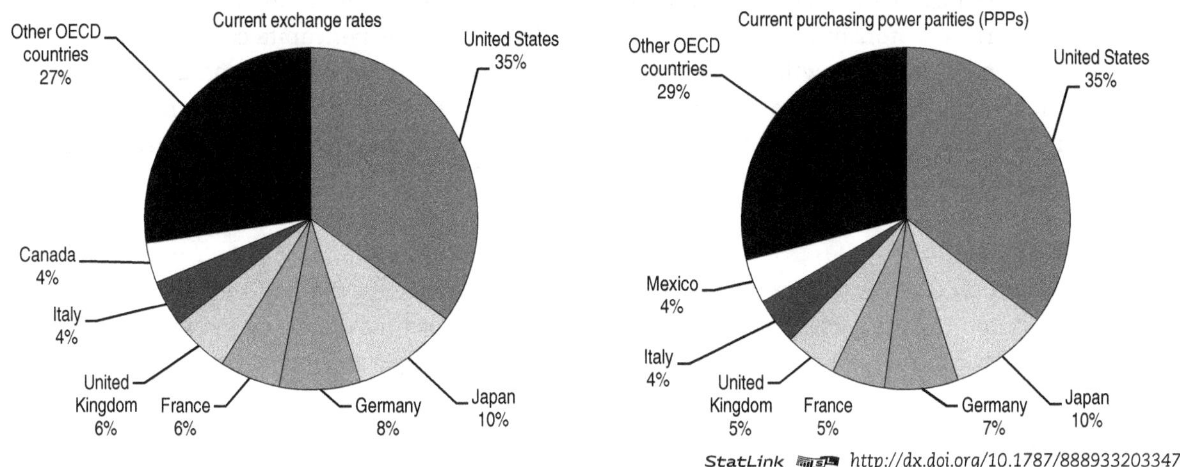

StatLink http://dx.doi.org/10.1787/888933203347

Figure 1.2. **Growth in gross domestic product**

Volume, percentage change at annual rate

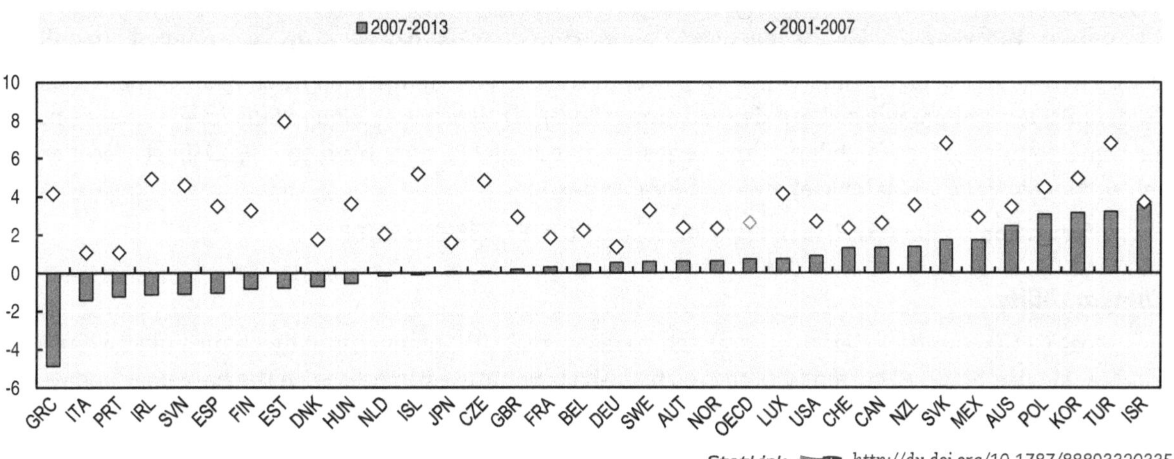

StatLink http://dx.doi.org/10.1787/888933203354

Figure 1.3. **GDP per capita**

US dollar per head of population, current prices and current PPPs, 2013

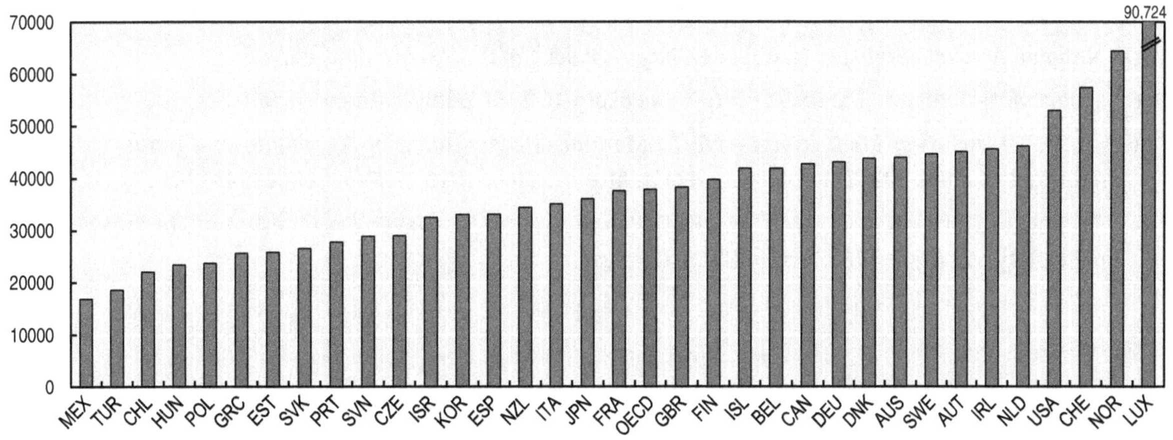

StatLink http://dx.doi.org/10.1787/888933203366

Growth in GDP per capita

Gross Domestic Product (GDP) per capita measures economic activity or income per person and is one of the core indicators of economic performance. Growth in GDP per capita can be broken down into a part which is due to growth in labour productivity (GDP per hour worked) and a part which is due to increased labour utilisation (hours worked per capita). A slowing or declining rate of labour utilisation combined with high labour productivity growth can be indicative of a greater use of capital and/or of structural shifts to higher-productivity activities.

Key facts

Differences in GDP per capita growth across OECD countries over the last two decades can be mainly attributed to differences in labour productivity growth, as measured by growth in GDP per hour worked. In contrast, labour utilisation has increased in only a few countries and at a much slower pace.

The picture has been more varied since the outset of the financial crisis in 2007. In some countries, declines in GDP per capita have gone hand-in-hand with substantial falls in labour utilisation rates.

Definition

Growth in GDP per capita is calculated using GDP and population estimates published in the *OECD National Accounts Statistics* (database). Labour utilisation is defined as hours worked per capita. By default, total hours worked are derived from the *OECD National Accounts Statistics* (database), but for some countries, for which long time series are not available, data from the *OECD Employment and Labour Market Statistics* (database) are used (see Annex B).

Information on data for Israel: *http://dx.doi.org/10.1787/888932315602*.

Comparability

Most OECD countries derive annual estimates of real GDP using annually chain-linked volume indices. Mexico however currently produces fixed-base volume estimates with the base year updated less periodically. The *System of National Accounts* recommends the production of estimates on the basis of annual chain volume series. These produce better estimates of growth as the weights used for the contribution of different goods and services are more relevant to the period in question.

Sources and further reading

OECD Employment and Labour Market Statistics (database), *http://dx.doi.org/10.1787/data-00303-en*.

OECD National Accounts Statistics (database), *http://dx.doi.org/10.1787/na-data-en*.

OECD Productivity Statistics (database), *http://dx.doi.org/10.1787/pdtvy-data-en*.

OECD (2001), *Measuring Productivity – OECD Manual: Measurement of Aggregate and Industry-level Productivity Growth*, OECD Publishing, Paris, *http://dx.doi.org/10.1787/9789264194519-en*.

Pilat, D. and P. Schreyer (2004), "The OECD Productivity Database: An Overview", *International Productivity Monitor*, No. 8, Spring, CSLS, Ottawa.

Figure 1.4. **Contributions to growth in GDP per capita**

Total economy, percentage change at annual rate

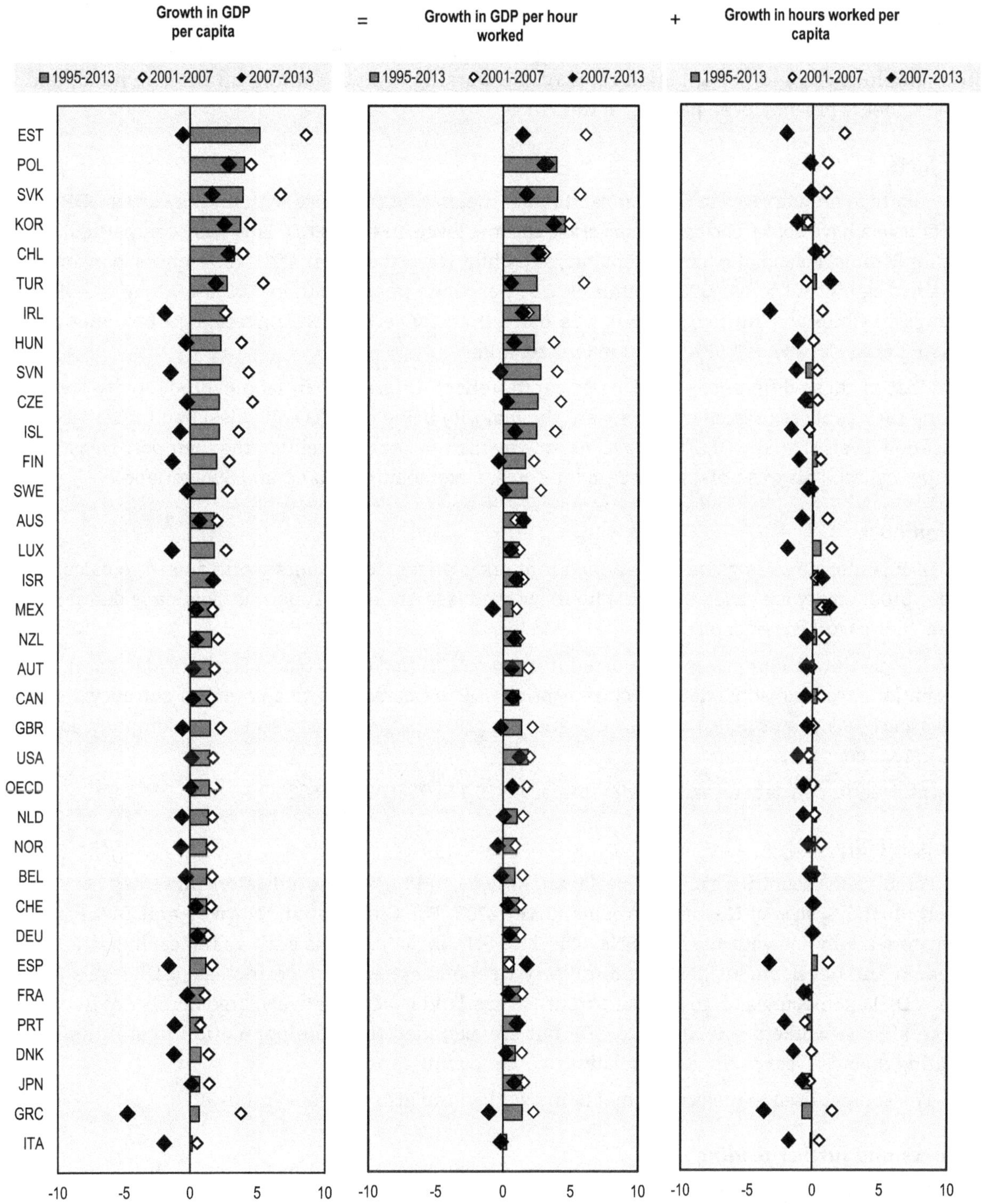

Growth in GDP per capita = Growth in GDP per hour worked + Growth in hours worked per capita

■1995-2013 ◇2001-2007 ◆2007-2013

EST, POL, SVK, KOR, CHL, TUR, IRL, HUN, SVN, CZE, ISL, FIN, SWE, AUS, LUX, ISR, MEX, NZL, AUT, CAN, GBR, USA, OECD, NLD, NOR, BEL, CHE, DEU, ESP, FRA, PRT, DNK, JPN, GRC, ITA

-10 -5 0 5 10

StatLink http://dx.doi.org/10.1787/888933203377

Gaps in GDP per capita

GDP per capita levels are typically used to compare living standards across countries. Differences in GDP per capita levels across countries can arise from differences in labour productivity levels and from differences in labour utilisation (hours worked per capita). The latter can represent differences in unemployment and participation rates of the working age population, on the one hand, and working hours per employed person, on the other.

Key facts

Very high growth rates in GDP per capita have meant that countries with initially lower GDP per capita levels have converged towards average income levels in the OECD. This has been particularly true for Estonia, Poland, the Slovak Republic, and Chile. Nevertheless, in 2013, differences in incomes remained significant across OECD countries. GDP per capita was more than 50% lower than the OECD average in Chile and Turkey, while it was more than twice the OECD average in Luxembourg, 70% higher in Norway and 52% higher in Switzerland.

Most of these differences in GDP per capita reflect differences in labour productivity levels. Among the countries presented, seventeen (the majority being non-EU countries) had higher labour utilisation levels than the OECD average, narrowing their negative or reinforcing their positive gap in GDP per capita. This was notably the case for Korea, Luxembourg, Iceland and Switzerland.

Definition

GDP is measured as gross value added in market prices. Total hours worked used to calculate labour productivity are based on actual hours worked (see Annex B). Labour utilisation is defined as actual hours worked per capita.

GDP data at current prices are sourced from the *OECD National Accounts Statistics* (database). For international comparisons, data on current price GDP are converted to a common currency, using *Purchasing Power Parities* (PPPs) as these measure the prices of the same basket of consumption goods in different countries.

Information on data for Israel: *http://dx.doi.org/10.1787/888932315602*.

Comparability

For all OECD countries except Chile, Japan, Norway and Turkey, the indicators presented here are based on the *System of National Accounts* (SNA) 2008. For Chile, Japan, Norway and Turkey the indicators are in line with the 1993 SNA. The 2008 SNA includes items such as the capitalisation of research and development (R&D) and military weapons systems which increase GDP levels (see Annex D). Luxembourg and, to a lesser extent, Switzerland have a relatively large number of frontier workers. Such workers contribute to GDP but are excluded from the population figures, and so inflating their GDP per capita levels relative to other countries.

The sources used to measure actual hours worked can also vary (see Annex B).

Sources and further reading

OECD National Accounts Statistics (database), *http://dx.doi.org/10.1787/na-data-en*.

OECD Productivity Statistics (database), *http://dx.doi.org/10.1787/pdtvy-data-en*.

OECD (2001), *Measuring Productivity – OECD Manual: Measurement of Aggregate and Industry-level Productivity Growth*, OECD Publishing, Paris, *http://dx.doi.org/10.1787/9789264194519-en*.

Figure 1.5. **Gaps in GDP per capita**

Percentage point differences, *vis-à-vis* the OECD

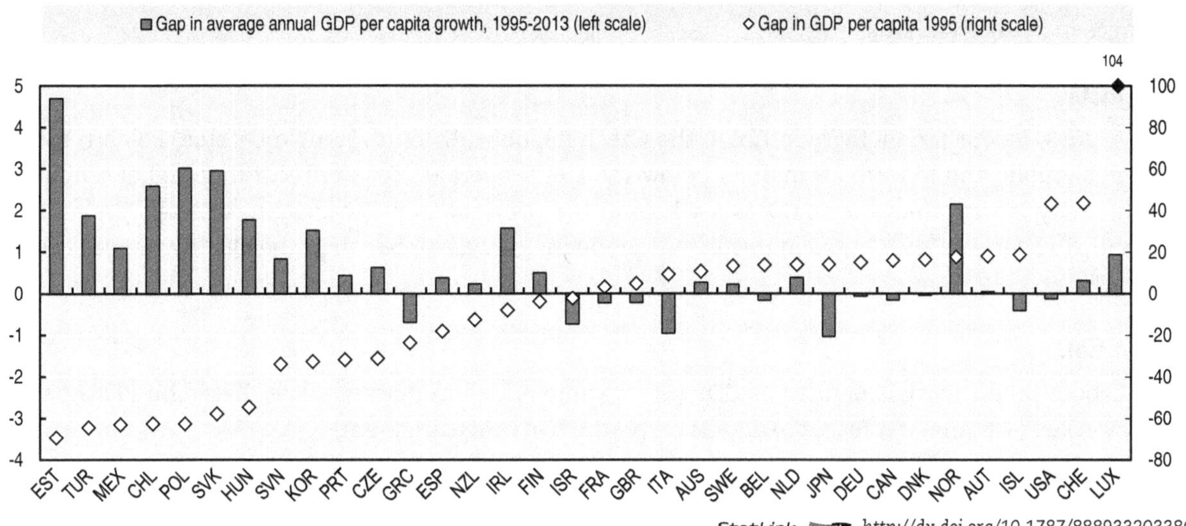

Gap in average annual GDP per capita growth, 1995-2013 (left scale)
Gap in GDP per capita 1995 (right scale)
104
5
4
3
2
1
0
-1
-2
-3
-4
100
80
60
40
20
0
-20
-40
-60
-80
EST
TUR
MEX
CHL
POL
SVK
HUN
SVN
KOR
PRT
CZE
GRC
ESP
NZL
IRL
FIN
ISR
FRA
GBR
ITA
AUS
SWE
BEL
NLD
JPN
DEU
CAN
DNK
NOR
AUT
ISL
USA
CHE
LUX

StatLink http://dx.doi.org/10.1787/888933203386

Figure 1.6. **Differences in GDP per capita levels, 2013**

Percentage differences *vis-à-vis* the OECD average, in current prices and current PPPs

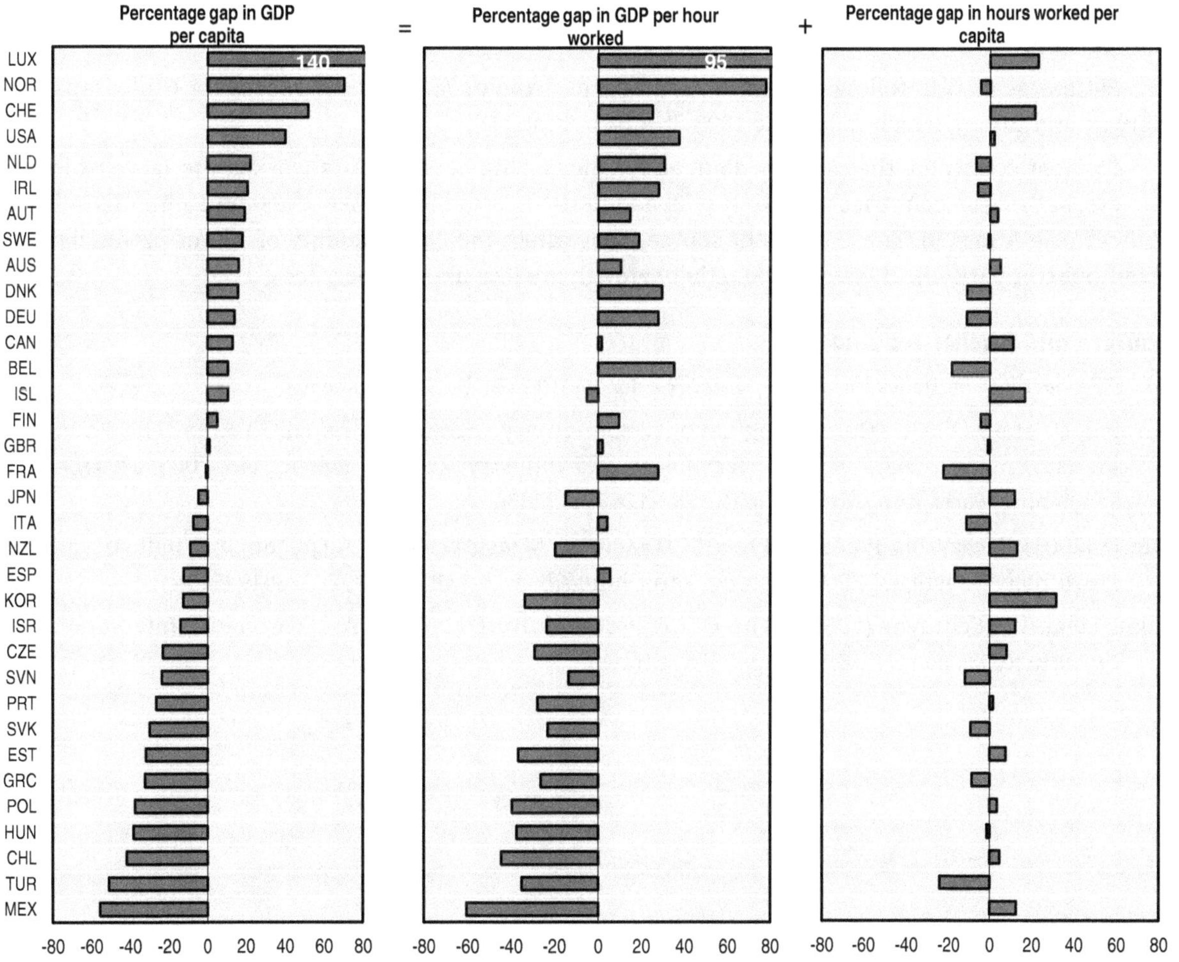

Percentage gap in GDP per capita
=
Percentage gap in GDP per hour worked
+
Percentage gap in hours worked per capita
140
95
LUX
NOR
CHE
USA
NLD
IRL
AUT
SWE
AUS
DNK
DEU
CAN
BEL
ISL
FIN
GBR
FRA
JPN
ITA
NZL
ESP
KOR
ISR
CZE
SVN
PRT
SVK
EST
GRC
POL
HUN
CHL
TUR
MEX
-80 -60 -40 -20 0 20 40 60 80
-80 -60 -40 -20 0 20 40 60 80
-80 -60 -40 -20 0 20 40 60 80

StatLink http://dx.doi.org/10.1787/888933203394

Labour productivity

Labour productivity is a key dimension of economic performance and an essential driver of changes in living standards.

Key facts

In 2013, labour productivity in Chile, the Czech Republic, Estonia, Hungary, Korea, Poland, the Slovak Republic and Slovenia remained below the OECD average, despite recording higher labour productivity growth than the OECD as a whole in the previous two decades. In Australia, Ireland, Finland, Sweden and the United States labour productivity was higher than the OECD average, and also grew at a higher rate.

Definition

Labour productivity is defined as GDP (Gross Value Added in market prices, based on PPPs) per hour worked (see Annex A for more details on productivity measurement).

Hours worked reflect regular hours worked by full-time and part-time workers, paid and unpaid overtime, hours worked in additional jobs, and time not worked because of public holidays, annual paid leaves, strikes and labour disputes, bad weather, economic conditions and other reasons (see Annex B).

Information on data for Israel: *http://dx.doi.org/10.1787/888932315602*.

Comparability

Estimates of GDP follow the *System of National Accounts* (SNA) 2008, except for Chile, Japan, Norway and Turkey, which follow the 1993 SNA (see Annex D).

In most countries, the primary sources for measuring actual hours worked are labour force surveys, but several countries rely – only or in addition – on establishment surveys and administrative sources (see Annex B). These different sources may affect the comparability of labour productivity levels but comparisons of labour productivity growth are less likely to be affected.

Sources and further reading

OECD Productivity Statistics (database), *http://dx.doi.org/10.1787/pdtvy-data-en*.

Ahmad, N. et al. (2003), "Comparing Labour Productivity Growth in the OECD Area: The Role of Measurement", *OECD Science, Technology and Industry Working Papers*, No. 2003/14, OECD Publishing, Paris, *http://dx.doi.org/10.1787/126534183836*.

OECD (2001), *Measuring Productivity – OECD Manual: Measurement of Aggregate and Industry-level Productivity Growth*, OECD Publishing, Paris, *http://dx.doi.org/10.1787/9789264194519-en*.

Pilat, D. and P. Schreyer (2004), "The OECD Productivity Database: An Overview", *International Productivity Monitor*, No. 8, Spring, CSLS, Ottawa.

Figure 1.7. **Labour productivity, 2013**

GDP per hour worked, total economy, US dollars, current prices and current PPPs

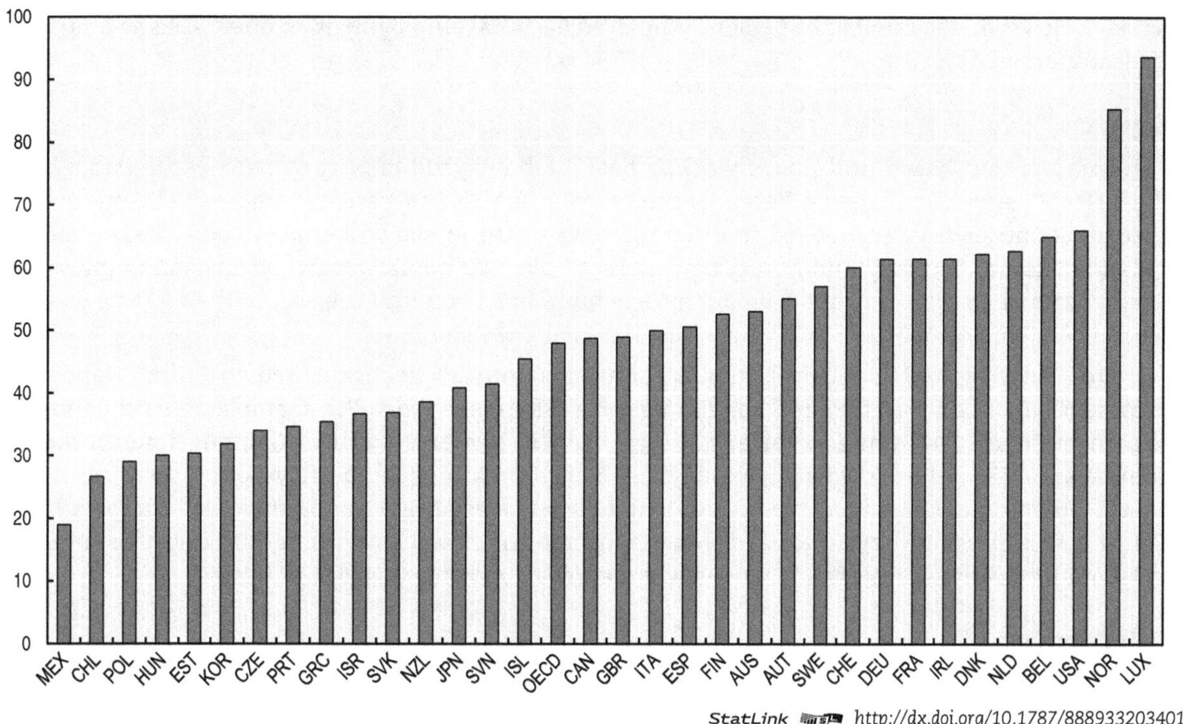

StatLink http://dx.doi.org/10.1787/888933203401

Figure 1.8. **Growth in labour productivity**

GDP per hour worked, total economy, percentage change at annual rate

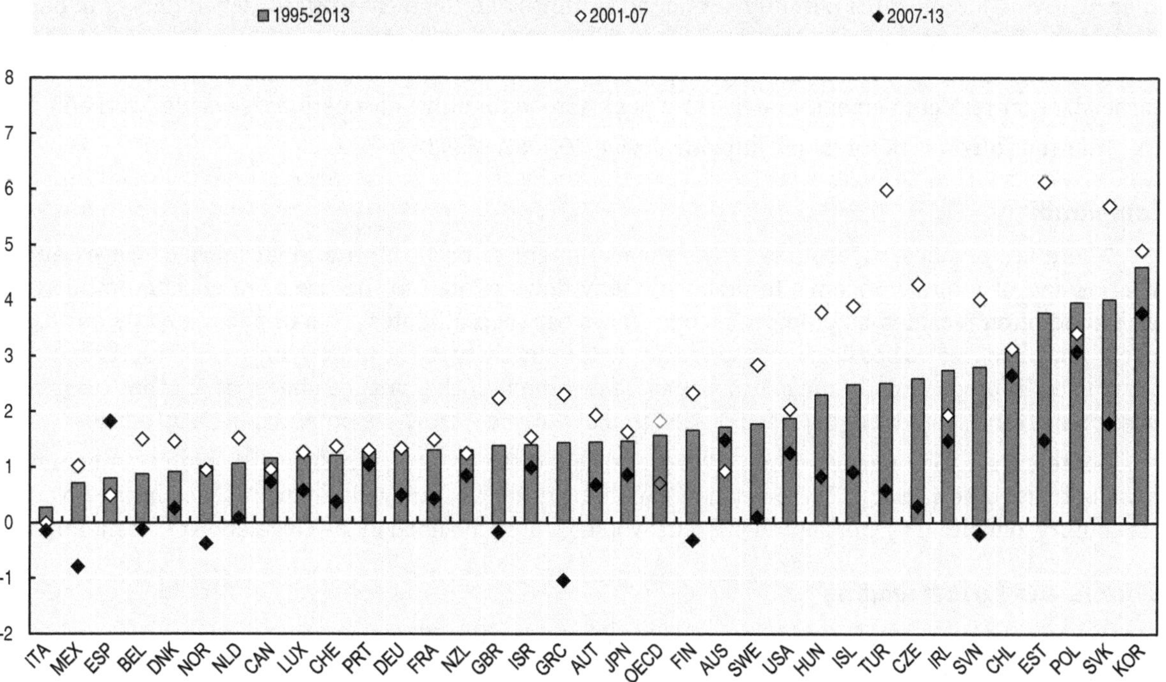

StatLink http://dx.doi.org/10.1787/888933203411

Alternative measures of labour productivity

Labour productivity is most appropriately measured as a volume of output generated per hour worked. However, the number of persons employed (i.e. total employment) is often used as a proxy for labour input.

Key facts

Employment based and hours worked based labour productivity growth estimates over the 2007-13 period show larger differences compared to the 2001-07 period for most OECD countries. Indeed, countries have responded in different ways to the crisis: while most countries, notably, Ireland, Estonia, Germany and Korea, have reduced average hours worked per person employee, Spain, Sweden, Luxembourg and Belgium have reduced head-counts. Care should therefore be taken when using employment as a proxy for measuring hours worked.

Productivity growth is relatively similar for most countries when measured on a Gross National Income (GNI) or GDP basis, even if some noticeable differences exist. For example, in both periods shown in Figure 1.10, Chile experienced significantly higher growth in GNI per hour worked compared to GDP per hour worked, possibly reflecting decreasing (net) outflows of property income. On the other hand, Ireland recorded consistently higher rates of GDP per hour worked compared to GNI, due to increasing (net) outflows of property income. In general however, the ranking of countries in labour productivity levels is unchanged whether measured on a GDP or GNI basis.

Definition

Total employment is measured as the total number of persons engaged in production (employees plus self-employed).

GNI is defined as GDP plus net receipts from abroad of wages and salaries and of property income plus net taxes and subsidies receivable from abroad. In most countries, net receipts of property income account for most of the difference between GDP and GNI. Property income from abroad includes interest, dividends and all or part of the retained earnings of foreign enterprises owned fully or in part by residents. Wages and salaries from abroad are those that are earned by residents who essentially live and consume inside the economic territory but work abroad. They also include wages and salaries earned by non-resident persons who live and work abroad for only short periods (seasonal workers).

Information on data for Israel: *http://dx.doi.org/10.1787/888932315602*.

Comparability

There are practical difficulties in the measurement of both international flows of wages and salaries and of property income. In practice, many flows related to the use of intellectual property assets are often recorded as property income flows between affiliates. This impacts directly on GDP levels but it also creates possible inconsistencies for productivity as the underlying intellectual property being used in production in one country may be recorded on the balance sheets of another country. Measures of labour productivity based on GNI in part "correct" for these potential inconsistencies.

Some care is also needed when interpreting productivity in countries with high numbers of cross-border workers. Labour compensation earned by these workers will not be included in the GNI of the country in which they work but their hours worked will be included in the calculation of labour input.

Sources and further reading

OECD National Accounts Statistics (database), *http://dx.doi.org/10.1787/na-data-en*.

OECD Productivity Statistics (database), *http://dx.doi.org/10.1787/pdtvy-data-en*.

Lequiller, F. and D. Blades (2007), *Understanding National Accounts*, OECD Publishing, Paris, *http://dx.doi.org/10.1787/9789264027657-en*.

OECD (2009), *Handbook on Deriving Capital Measures of Intellectual Property Products*, OECD Publishing, Paris, *http://dx.doi.org/10.1787/9789264079205-en*.

Figure 1.9. **Growth in GDP per hour worked and growth in GDP per person employed**

Total economy, percentage change at annual rate

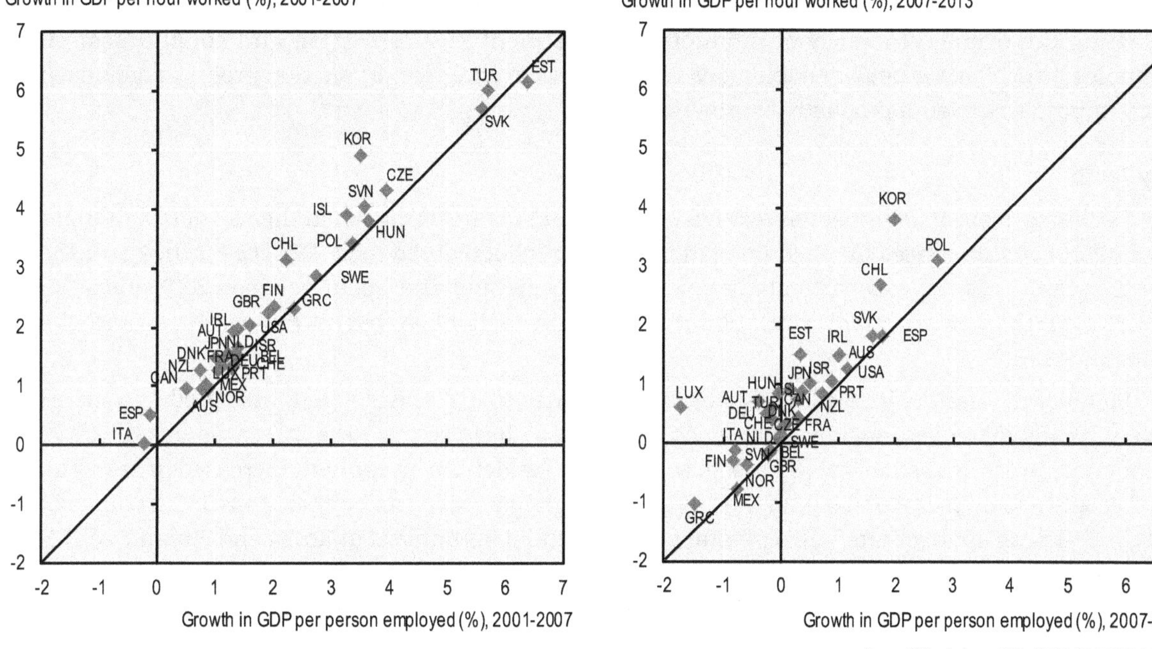

StatLink http://dx.doi.org/10.1787/888933203421

Figure 1.10. **Growth in GDP per hour worked and growth in GNI per hour worked**

Total economy, percentage change at annual rate

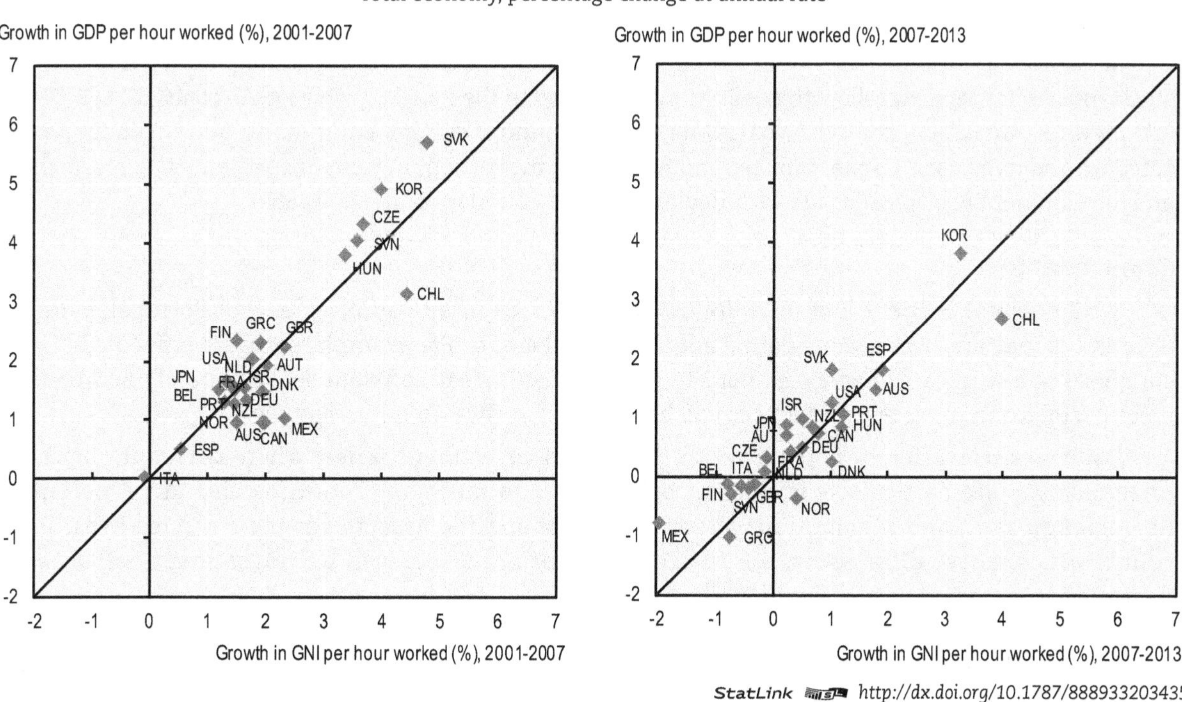

StatLink http://dx.doi.org/10.1787/888933203435

Capital productivity

Capital productivity shows how efficiently capital is used to generate output. It reflects the joint influence of labour input per unit of capital used and multifactor productivity (MFP); the latter reflecting the overall efficiency of production. Investment in information and communication technologies (ICT) in particular enables new technologies to enter the production process and is seen as an important driver of productivity growth.

Key facts

Declining costs of using capital relative to labour and the resulting fall in the use of labour input per unit of capital services have led to a fall in capital productivity in most OECD countries over the past 15 years. This fall was particularly pronounced in Ireland and Spain between 2007 and 2013, while, over the same period, a relative improvement was observed in Japan, Korea and the United States.

Some of the decline in overall costs of capital relates to ICT assets where new products' prices have typically fallen very rapidly, and which in turn may have spurred the increased use of ICT in production. In fact, the shares of ICT assets in total non-residential investment increased in nearly all OECD countries in the second half of the 1990s, although have fallen since then. In 2013, the share of ICT ranged from approximately 10% of total non-residential investment in Korea and Finland, to 20% in Denmark and one quarter in New Zealand. In Australia, shares fell significantly between 2001 and 2013, partly reflecting significant investment in mining capital equipment.

Definition

Capital productivity is measured as the ratio between the volume of output (GDP), and the volume of capital input, defined as the flow of productive services that capital delivers in production, i.e. capital services (see Annexes A and C).

Measures of investment (gross fixed capital formation) used to estimate the productive capital stock and capital services follow the definitions described in the *System of National Accounts* (SNA) 2008. ICT products include: i) computer hardware; ii) telecommunications equipment; and iii) computer software and databases. Capital input estimates include investment in weapons systems and research and development (R&D), which are included in the asset boundary of the 2008 SNA.

Comparability

While capital services measures follow the 2008 SNA in all countries except Portugal, some differences may arise when considering specific capital assets. For example, software embodied in a computer will be recorded as investment in computers whereas software sold separately and then installed on a computer by an end-user will be recorded as investment in software.

Countries use different approaches to deflate ICT investment series; where constant quality price changes are particularly important but difficult to measure. Countries also use different depreciation rates and assumptions about the use of specific assets over their service lives. To counteract for these differences, the OECD uses a set of harmonised ICT investment deflators, depreciation rates and service lives for all assets.

Sources and further reading

OECD Productivity Statistics (database), *http://dx.doi.org/10.1787/pdtvy-data-en.*

OECD (2009), *Measuring Capital – OECD Manual 2009: Second edition*, OECD Publishing, Paris, *http://dx.doi.org/10.1787/9789264068476-en.*

Schreyer, P. (2004), "Capital Stocks, Capital Services and Multi-Factor Productivity Measures", *OECD Economic Studies*, Vol. 2003/2, OECD Publishing, Paris, *http://dx.doi.org/10.1787/eco_studies-v2003-art11-en.*

Figure 1.11. **Growth in capital productivity**

Total economy, percentage change at annual rate

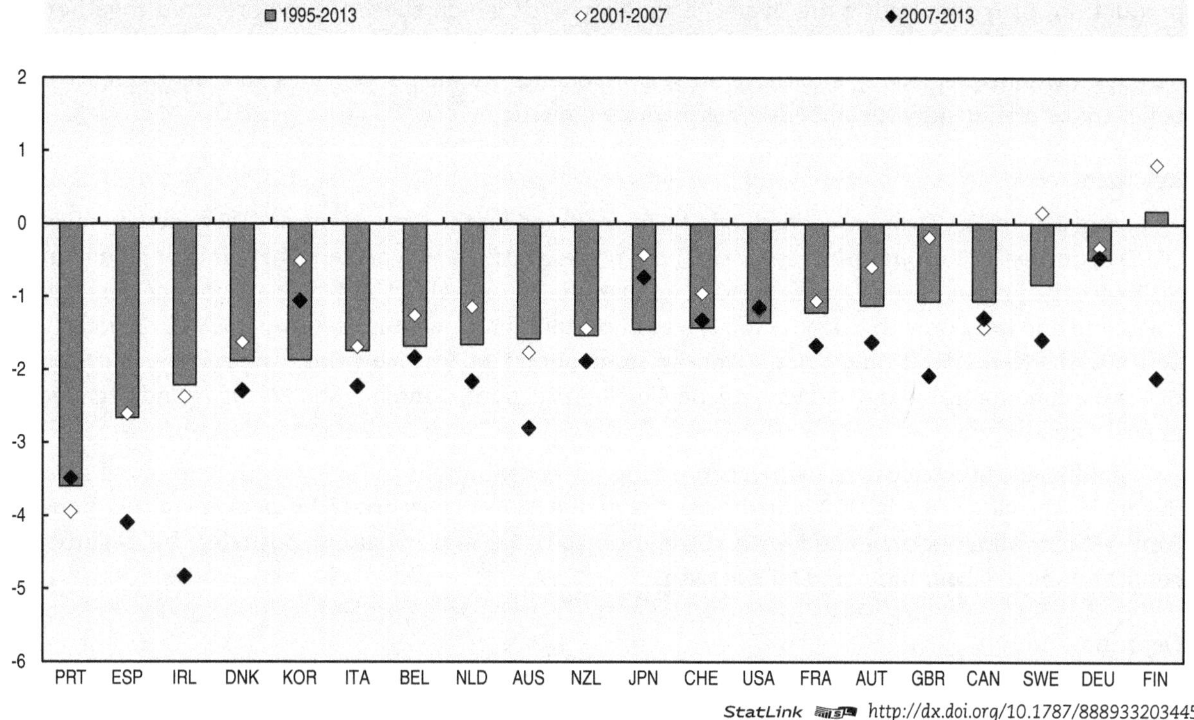

StatLink http://dx.doi.org/10.1787/888933203445

Figure 1.12. **Share of ICT investment**

Total economy, as a percentage of non-residential gross fixed capital formation

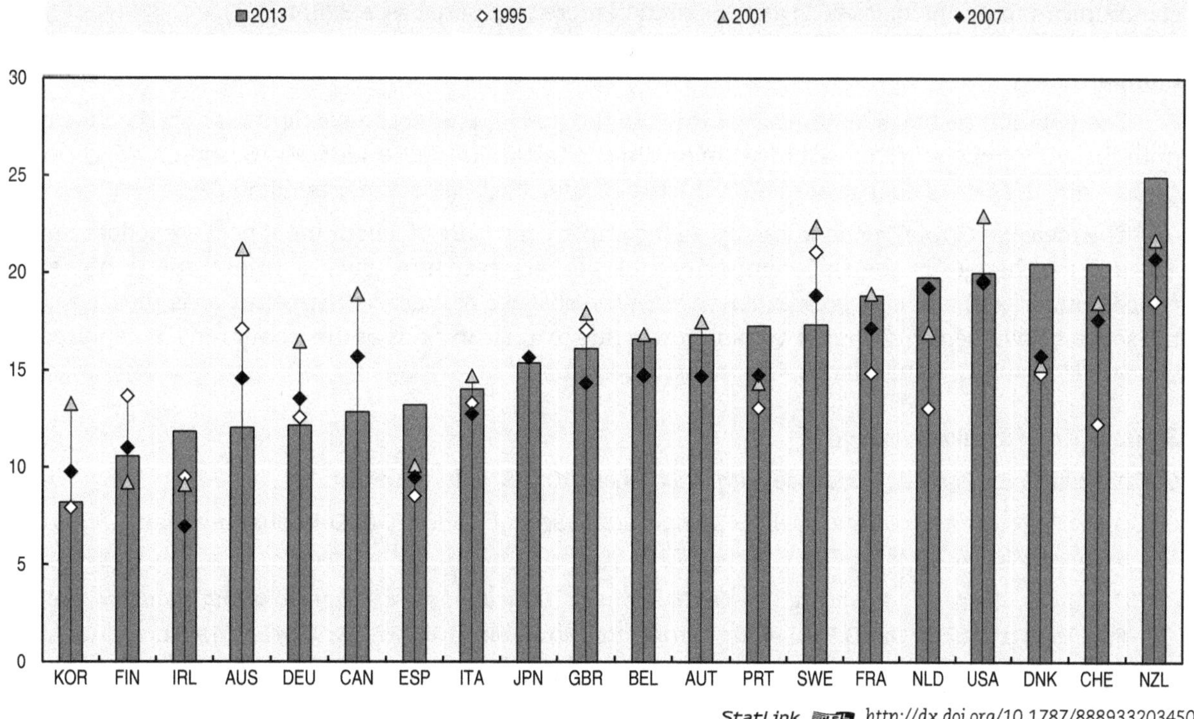

StatLink http://dx.doi.org/10.1787/888933203450

Growth accounting

Economic growth can be fostered either by raising the labour and capital inputs used in production, or by improving the overall efficiency with which these inputs are used together, i.e. higher multifactor productivity growth (MFP). Growth accounting involves decomposing total output growth, (GDP growth), into these three components. As such, it provides an essential tool for policy makers to identify the underlying drivers for growth.

Key facts

From 1995 to 2013, capital services and MFP accounted for the largest part of GDP growth in most OECD countries. ICT capital services represented between 0.2 and 0.6 percentage points of growth in GDP, with the largest contributions recorded in Australia, New Zealand and Sweden, and the smallest in Finland and Italy. Growth in labour input was important for a few countries over 1995-2013, notably Belgium, the Netherlands and Spain. Over the same period, MFP growth was a significant source of GDP growth in Korea, Ireland and Finland, negligible in Belgium, Denmark and Portugal, and negative in Spain and Italy.

Significant differences arise when comparing the contributions to GDP growth before and after the crisis. The slowdown in GDP growth over the period 2007-13 was driven by weaker contributions from all components compared with the period 2001-07, and in many countries, by negative contributions of labour input and MFP growth.

Definition

Total output growth can be decomposed into a labour input component, a capital input component and multifactor productivity (MFP) growth, computed as a residual (see Annex A). The contribution of labour (capital) to GDP growth is measured as the growth in labour (capital) input, multiplied by the share of labour (capital) in total costs. In the figures below, the contribution of capital to GDP growth is further broken down to highlight the contribution made by information and communication technologies (ICT) as compared to more traditional assets (non-ICT).

Comparability

The appropriate measure for capital input is the flow of productive services that can be drawn from the cumulative stock of past investments in capital assets. These services are estimated by the OECD using the rate of change of the "productive capital stock" (see Annexes A and C).

The measure of total hours worked is an incomplete measure of labour input because it does not account for changes in the skill composition of workers over time, such as those due to higher educational attainment and work experience. In the absence of these adjustments, as is the case in the series shown here, more rapid output growth due to a rise in skills of the labour force is captured by the MFP residual, rather than being attributed to labour.

Sources and further reading

OECD *Productivity Statistics* (database), *http://dx.doi.org/10.1787/pdtvy-data-en.*

OECD (2009), *Measuring Capital – OECD Manual 2009: Second edition*, OECD Publishing, Paris, *http://dx.doi.org/10.1787/9789264068476-en.*

OECD (2001), *Measuring Productivity – OECD Manual: Measurement of Aggregate and Industry-level Productivity Growth*, OECD Publishing, Paris, *http://dx.doi.org/10.1787/9789264194519-en.*

Schreyer, P. (2004), "Capital Stocks, Capital Services and Multi-Factor Productivity Measures", *OECD Economic Studies*, Vol. 2003/2, OECD Publishing, Paris, *http://dx.doi.org/10.1787/eco_studies-v2003-art11-en.*

Wölfl, A. and D. Hajkova (2007), "Measuring Multifactor Productivity Growth", *OECD Science, Technology and Industry Working Papers*, No. 2007/05, OECD Publishing, Paris, *http://dx.doi.org/10.1787/246367010342.*

Figure 1.13. **Contributions to GDP growth**

Total economy, annual percentage point contribution

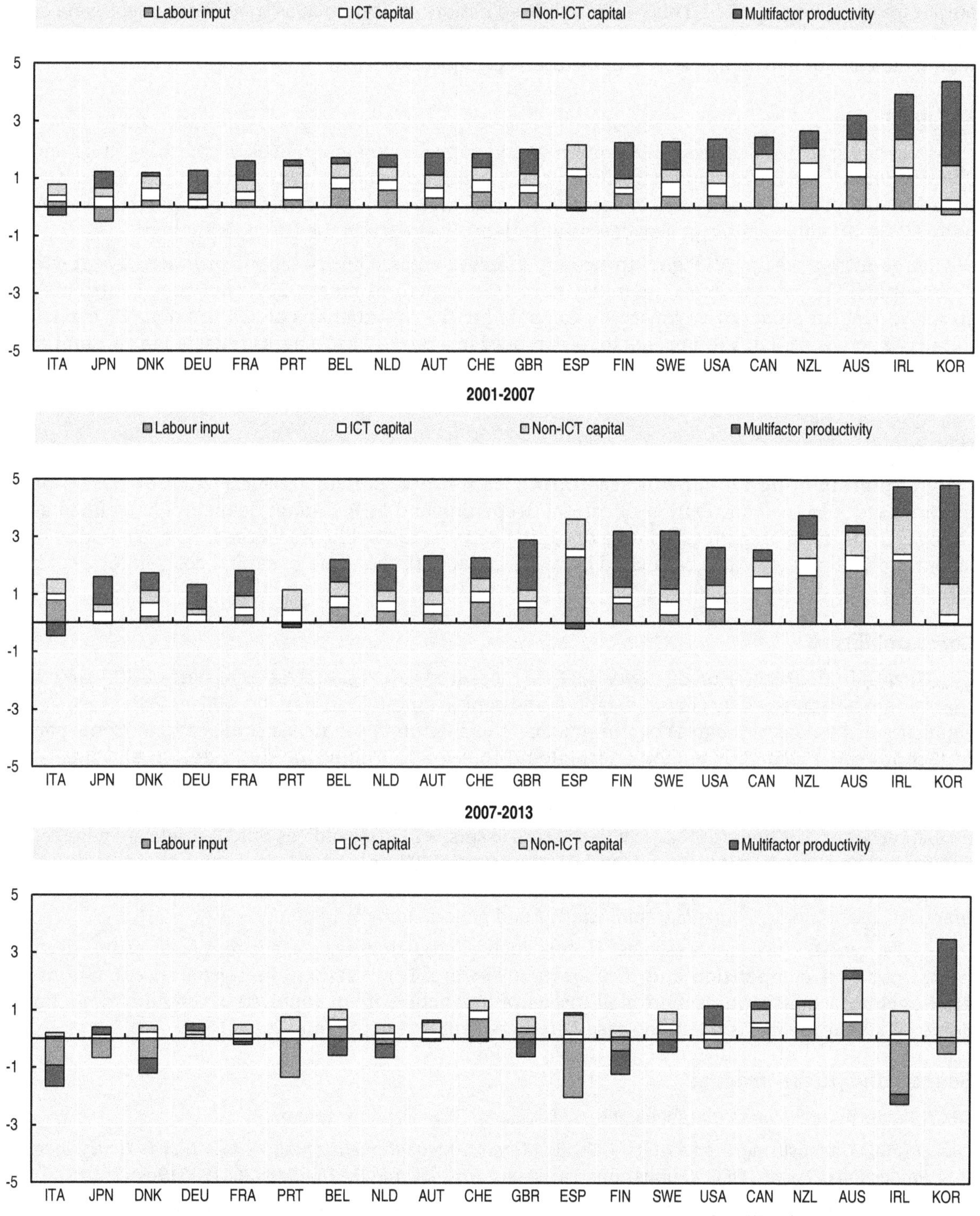

StatLink http://dx.doi.org/10.1787/888933203463

Multifactor productivity

Multifactor productivity (MFP) reflects the overall efficiency with which labour and capital inputs are used together in the production process. Labour productivity growth represents a higher level of output for every hour worked. This can be achieved if more capital, such as machinery or software or better vintages of it (capital deepening) is used in production, or by improving the overall efficiency with which labour and capital are used together, i.e. higher MFP.

Key facts

Over the last two decades, MFP growth varied considerably among OECD countries. Italy and Spain recorded the lowest (and negative) rates, lagging far behind the top performers Korea and Ireland. MFP growth decelerated in nearly all countries after the crisis as compared with the period 2001-07, with significant slowdowns in Finland, Sweden and the United Kingdom.

Large differences in MFP growth heavily affected cross-country labour productivity growth differentials. Prior to the crisis, relatively high MFP growth in most OECD countries contributed strongly to labour productivity growth, as compared to the contributions of ICT and non-ICT capital. In the post-crisis period, MFP appears to have moved in a pro-cyclical way, as reflected in substantial falls in MFP growth and the negligible or negative contributions to labour productivity growth in nearly all OECD countries.

Definition

By reformulating the growth accounting framework, labour productivity growth can be decomposed into the contribution of capital deepening and MFP. Capital deepening is defined as changes in the ratio of the total volume of capital services to total hours worked. Its contribution to labour productivity growth is calculated by weighting it with the share of capital costs in total costs (see Annex A).

Comparability

Growth in multifactor productivity (MFP) is measured as a residual, i.e. that part of GDP growth that cannot be explained by growth in labour and capital inputs. Traditionally, MFP growth is seen as capturing technological progress but, in practice, this interpretation needs some caution. Some part of technological change is embodied in capital input, e.g. improvements in design and quality between two vintages of the same capital asset, and so its effects on GDP growth are attributed to the respective factor. The measure of capital services in the *OECD Productivity Statistics* (database) takes explicit account of different productivities across assets, and price indices of ICT assets are adjusted for quality changes (see Annexes A and C). Therefore, MFP only picks up disembodied technical change, e.g. network effects or spillovers from production factors, the effects of better management practices, brand names, organisational change and general knowledge.

Moreover, MFP also captures other factors such as adjustment costs, economies of scale, effects from imperfect competition and measurement errors. For instance, increases in educational attainment or a shift towards more skill-intensive production, if not captured in the form of quality adjusted labour input – as is still the case here – are captured within measured MFP.

Sources and further reading

OECD *Productivity Statistics* (database), *http://dx.doi.org/10.1787/pdtvy-data-en*.

OECD (2001), *Measuring Productivity – OECD Manual: Measurement of Aggregate and Industry-level Productivity Growth*, OECD Publishing, Paris, *http://dx.doi.org/10.1787/9789264194519-en*.

Schreyer, P. (2004), "Capital Stocks, Capital Services and Multi-Factor Productivity Measures", *OECD Economic Studies*, Vol. 2003/2, OECD Publishing, Paris, *http://dx.doi.org/10.1787/eco_studies-v2003-art11-en*.

Wölfl, A. and D. Hajkova (2007), "Measuring Multifactor Productivity Growth", *OECD Science, Technology and Industry Working Papers*, No. 2007/05, OECD Publishing, Paris, *http://dx.doi.org/10.1787/246367010342*.

Figure 1.14. Multifactor productivity growth

Total economy, percentage change at annual rate

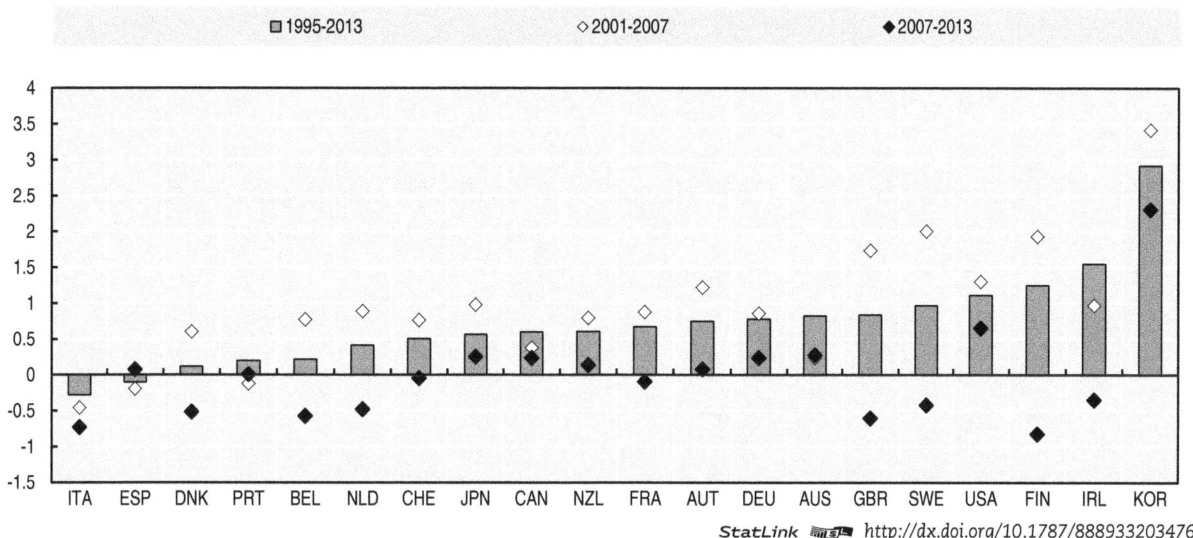

1995-2013
2001-2007
2007-2013
4
3.5
3
2.5
2
1.5
1
0.5
0
-0.5
-1
-1.5
ITA ESP DNK PRT BEL NLD CHE JPN CAN NZL FRA AUT DEU AUS GBR SWE USA FIN IRL KOR

StatLink http://dx.doi.org/10.1787/888933203476

Figure 1.15. Contributions to labour productivity growth

Total economy, annual percentage point contribution

2001-2007

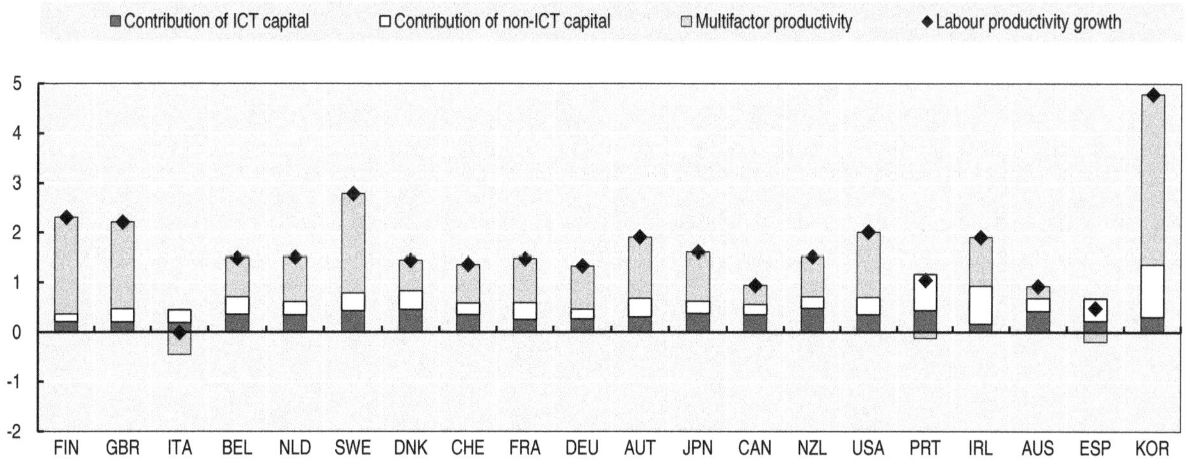

Contribution of ICT capital
Contribution of non-ICT capital
Multifactor productivity
Labour productivity growth
5
4
3
2
1
0
-1
-2
FIN GBR ITA BEL NLD SWE DNK CHE FRA DEU AUT JPN CAN NZL USA PRT IRL AUS ESP KOR

2007-2013

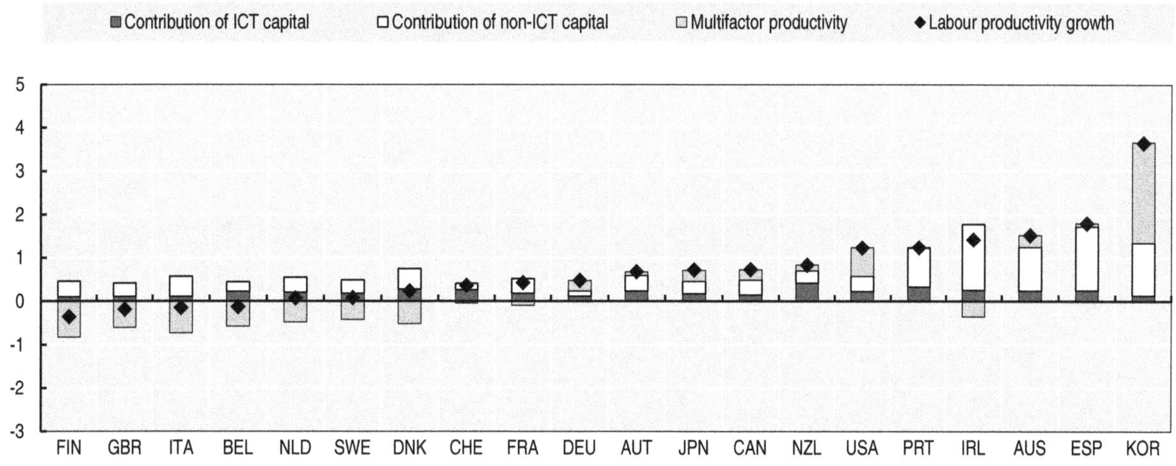

Contribution of ICT capital
Contribution of non-ICT capital
Multifactor productivity
Labour productivity growth
5
4
3
2
1
0
-1
-2
-3
FIN GBR ITA BEL NLD SWE DNK CHE FRA DEU AUT JPN CAN NZL USA PRT IRL AUS ESP KOR

StatLink http://dx.doi.org/10.1787/888933203483

OECD Compendium of Productivity Indicators 2015

Chapter 2

Productivity by industry

Labour productivity by main economic activity

Industry contribution to business sector productivity

Labour productivity of business sector services

Contributions to business sector services' productivity

Labour productivity by main economic activity

Sectors differ from each other with respect to their productivity growth. Such differences may relate, for instance, to the intensity with which sectors use capital and skilled labour in their production; the scope for product and process innovation and the absorption of external knowledge; the degree of product standardisation; the scope for economies of scale; and the exposure to international competition.

Key facts

Differences in productivity growth rates across countries are more evident when compared at the sectoral level. Although in most countries, the highest growth rates are typically in the manufacturing sector and in some business sector services, productivity growth rates can differ considerably. For instance, between 2001 and 2013, in manufacturing, productivity growth rates ranged from less than 1% in Italy to 11% in the Slovak Republic. For most OECD countries, annual labour productivity growth in all sectors has been significantly lower since the crisis.

Definition

Labour productivity is defined as real value added per hour worked. The non-agricultural business sector, excluding real estate covers mining and quarrying; manufacturing; utilities; construction; and business sector services. The latter cover wholesale and retail trade, repair; accommodation, food services, and transport services; information and communication; financial and insurance activities; professional, scientific and support activities. Figure 2.1 presents sectoral productivity growth for those countries for which sectoral data for real value added (in basic prices) and hours worked are available by ISIC Rev. 4 breakdown in the *OECD National Accounts Statistics* (database).

Information on data for Israel: *http://dx.doi.org/10.1787/888932315602*.

Comparability

The comparability of productivity growth across industries and countries may be affected by problems in measuring real value added, especially in services (Annex E). Most countries assume no change in labour productivity for public administration activities, which is why this industry is not included here. Also excluded are real estate services, as their value-added includes the imputation made for the dwelling services provided and consumed by home-owners.

Sources and further reading

OECD National Accounts Statistics (database), *http://dx.doi.org/10.1787/na-data-en*.

OECD Productivity Statistics (database), *http://dx.doi.org/10.1787/pdtvy-data-en*.

Ahmad, N. et al. (2003), "Comparing Labour Productivity Growth in the OECD Area: The Role of Measurement", *OECD Science, Technology and Industry Working Papers*, No. 2003/14, OECD Publishing, Paris, *http://dx.doi.org/10.1787/126534183836*.

OECD (2001), *Measuring Productivity – OECD Manual: Measurement of Aggregate and Industry-level Productivity Growth*, OECD Publishing, Paris, *http://dx.doi.org/10.1787/9789264194519-en*.

Wölfl, A. (2003), "Productivity Growth in Services Industries: An Assessment of Recent Patterns and the Role of Measurement", *OECD Science, Technology and Industry Working Papers*, No. 2003/07, OECD Publishing, Paris, *http://dx.doi.org/10.1787/086461104618*.

Figure 2.1. **Labour productivity by main activity**

Real value added per hour worked, percentage change at annual rate

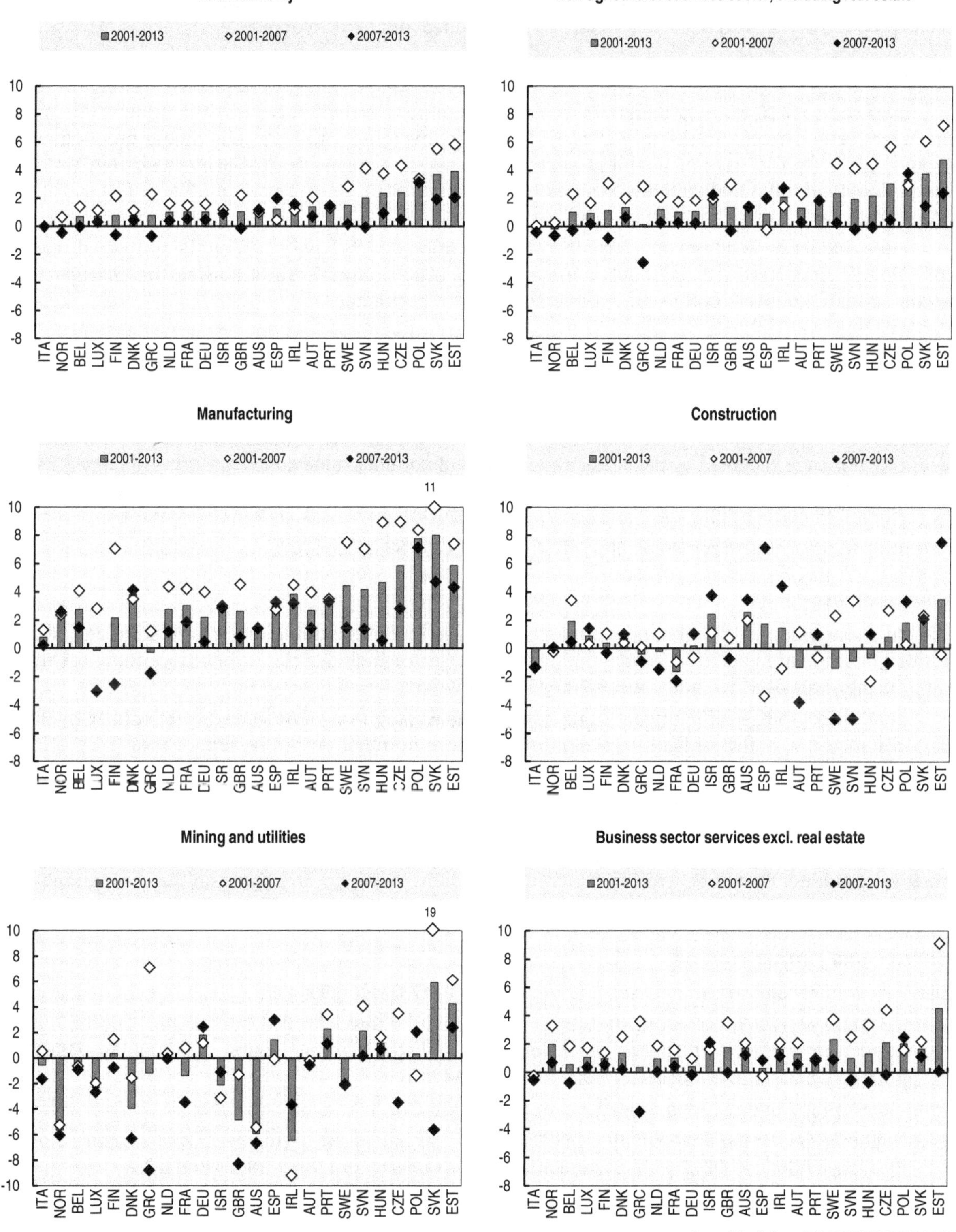

StatLink http://dx.doi.org/10.1787/888933203498

Industry contribution to business sector productivity

Understanding the drivers of productivity growth in the business sector requires an understanding of the contribution that each industry makes. The contribution of an individual sector depends not only on its productivity growth but also its share of value added and hours worked.

Key facts

Over the past 10 years, productivity growth was almost entirely driven by manufacturing and business sector services. In the case of manufacturing, this reflects the typically higher productivity growth rates. In the case of business sector services, the strong contribution also reveals its increasing share of overall activity. Business sector services make up between 50 and 70% of total employment and value added across OECD countries.

The evidence available so far suggests that reallocation effects have not been the primary drivers for overall labour productivity movements since the 2008 financial crisis. Rather, the changes in sector contributions reflect those in productivity growth per sector.

Definition

Labour productivity growth per industry is defined as the rate of change of real value added (in basic prices) per hour worked. The contribution of each sector to labour productivity growth of the total business sector is computed as the difference between the growth rate of value added and that of hours worked, with each weighted by the sector's share in total nominal value added and total hours worked respectively. Data are presented for those countries for which data for real value added and hours worked by sector are available by ISIC Rev. 4 breakdown in the *OECD National Accounts Statistics* (database).

Information on data for Israel: *http://dx.doi.org/10.1787/888932315602*.

Comparability

Business sector refers to non-agricultural business sector excluding real estate activities. Real estate activities are excluded as value-added in this sector includes the imputation made for the dwelling services provided and consumed by home-owners.

In addition to the difficulties encountered in measuring real value added, particularly in the services sector, it is also difficult to accurately measure nominal output in some cases. This is for example the case for the financial services sector, where some financial intermediation services, such as implicit banking charges, are indirectly measured.

Under- or over-estimation of the output of a particular sector, notably for services, will be partially offset by intermediate consumption of this output by other production sectors, and hence their value added. Therefore, while this mis-measurement may have an impact on the comparability across sectors it may have a smaller impact on overall productivity growth.

Sources and further reading

OECD Productivity Statistics (database), *http://dx.doi.org/10.1787/pdtvy-data-en*.

Ahmad, N. et al. (2003), "Comparing Labour Productivity Growth in the OECD Area: The Role of Measurement", *OECD Science, Technology and Industry Working Papers*, No. 2003/14, OECD Publishing, Paris, *http://dx.doi.org/10.1787/126534183836*.

Inter-Secretariat Working Group on National Accounts (ISWGNA), Task Force on FISIM (2013), *Final Report*.

OECD (2001), *Measuring Productivity – OECD Manual: Measurement of Aggregate and Industry-level Productivity Growth*, OECD Publishing, Paris, *http://dx.doi.org/10.1787/9789264194519-en*.

Pilat, D. and A. Wölfl (2005), "Measuring the Interaction between Manufacturing and Services", *OECD Science, Technology and Industry Working Papers*, No. 2005/05, OECD Publishing, Paris, *http://dx.doi.org/10.1787/882376471514*.

Wölfl, A. (2003), "Productivity Growth in Services Industries: An Assessment of Recent Patterns and the Role of Measurement", *OECD Science, Technology and Industry Working Papers*, No. 2003/07, OECD Publishing, Paris, *http://dx.doi.org/10.1787/086461104618*.

Figure 2.2. **Industry contribution to business sector productivity growth**

Real value added per hour worked, percentage point contribution at annual rate

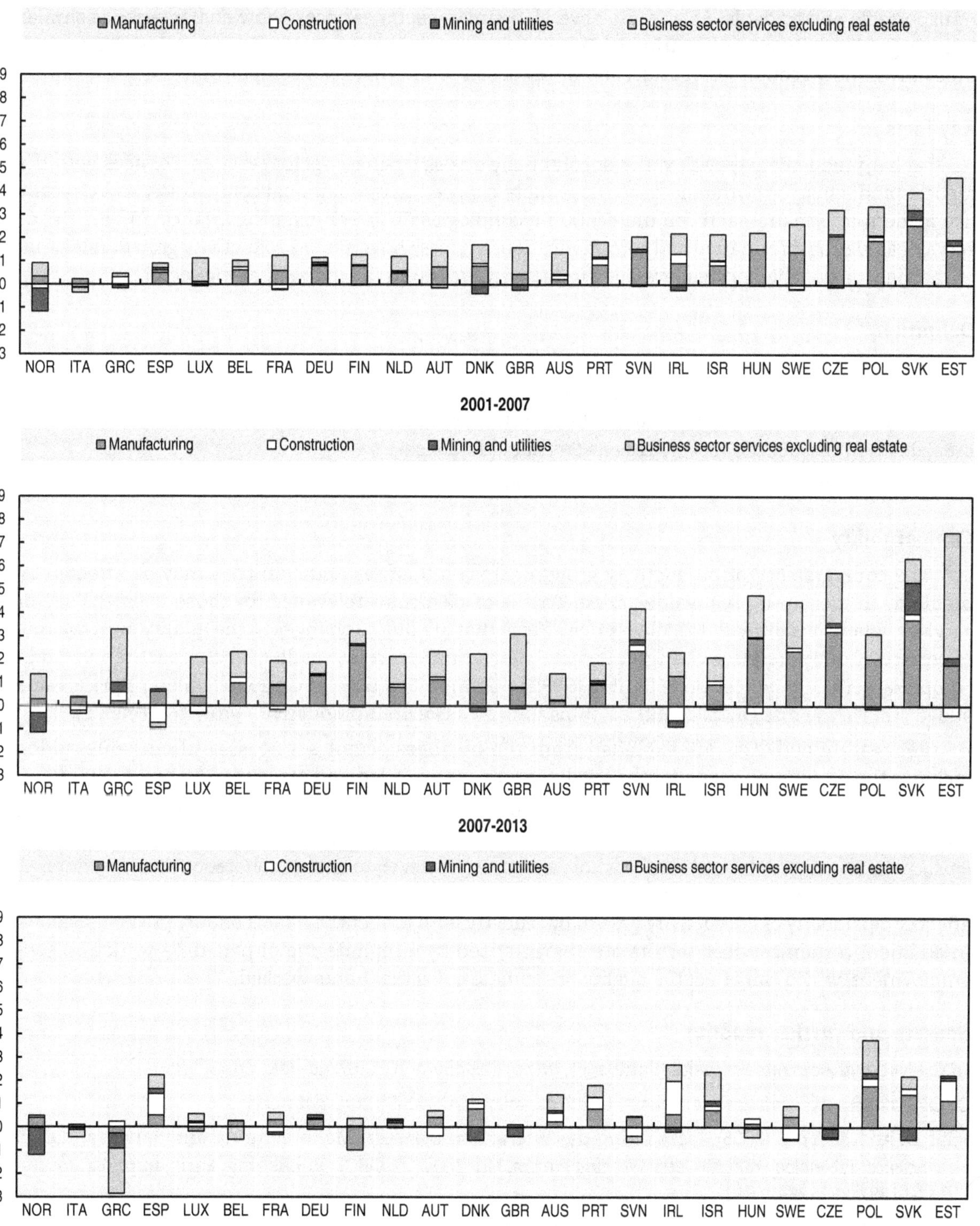

StatLink http://dx.doi.org/10.1787/888933203507

Labour productivity of business sector services

Developments in information and telecommunications technologies (ICT) combined with internationally fragmented production processes are making business services increasingly dynamic, transportable and tradable. As a result, several business sector services show characteristics similar to high-productivity manufacturing industries; they are intensive in physical, notably ICT-capital, innovative, show economies of scale, and are exposed to international competition.

Key facts

Labour productivity growth varies substantially across business sector services. Services with the highest productivity growth tend to be those more exposed to international competition and typically use modern information and communication technologies (ICT). For instance, finance and insurance services as well as information and communication services show labour productivity growth rates that are as high, or even higher than average productivity growth in the manufacturing sector.

Definition

Labour productivity growth by industry is defined as the rate of growth in real value added (in basic prices) per hour worked by industry. The figures present sectoral productivity growth for those countries for which data for real value added and hours worked by sector are available by ISIC Rev. 4 breakdown in the *OECD National Accounts Statistics* (database).

Information on data for Israel: *http://dx.doi.org/10.1787/888932315602*.

Comparability

The comparability of productivity growth across industries and countries may be affected by problems in measuring real value added. This is of particular relevance for those business sector services, where it is difficult to isolate price effects that are due to changes in the quality or in the mix of services from pure price changes. Despite substantial progress made over the past ten years in compiling service producer price indices (SPPIs), the methods used to compute constant price value added still vary across OECD countries, impacting on measured productivity growth (Annex E).

Real estate activities are excluded from the business sector services, as their value-added includes the imputation made for the dwelling services provided and consumed by home-owners.

For some countries, labour force surveys (LFS) provide long time series for hours worked data at the total economy level, and hence for these countries, LFS data for hours worked are used in the *OECD Productivity Statistics* (database) for the whole economy. However, to ensure coherence across sectors, all sectoral hours worked data are taken from the *OECD National Accounts Statistics* (database). This can affect comparability of productivity growth by industry with that of the total economy presented above. In addition, certain services sectors are characterised by a high degree of part-time work and self-employment, which can affect the quality of estimates of actual hours worked.

Sources and further reading

OECD National Accounts Statistics (database), *http://dx.doi.org/10.1787/na-data-en*.

OECD Productivity Statistics (database), *http://dx.doi.org/10.1787/pdtvy-data-en*.

Pilat, D. and A. Wölfl (2005), "Measuring the Interaction between Manufacturing and Services", *OECD Science, Technology and Industry Working Papers*, No. 2005/05, OECD Publishing, Paris, *http://dx.doi.org/10.1787/882376471514*.

Wölfl, A. (2005), "The Service Economy in OECD Countries: OECD/Centre d'études prospectives et d'informations internationales (CEPII)", *OECD Science, Technology and Industry Working Papers*, No. 2005/03, *http://dx.doi.org/10.1787/212257000720*.

Wölfl, A. (2003), "Productivity Growth in Services Industries: An Assessment of Recent Patterns and the Role of Measurement", *OECD Science, Technology and Industry Working Papers*, No. 2003/07, OECD Publishing, Paris, *http://dx.doi.org/10.1787/086461104618*.

Figure 2.3. **Labour productivity by business sector services**

Real value added per hour worked, percentage change at annual rate

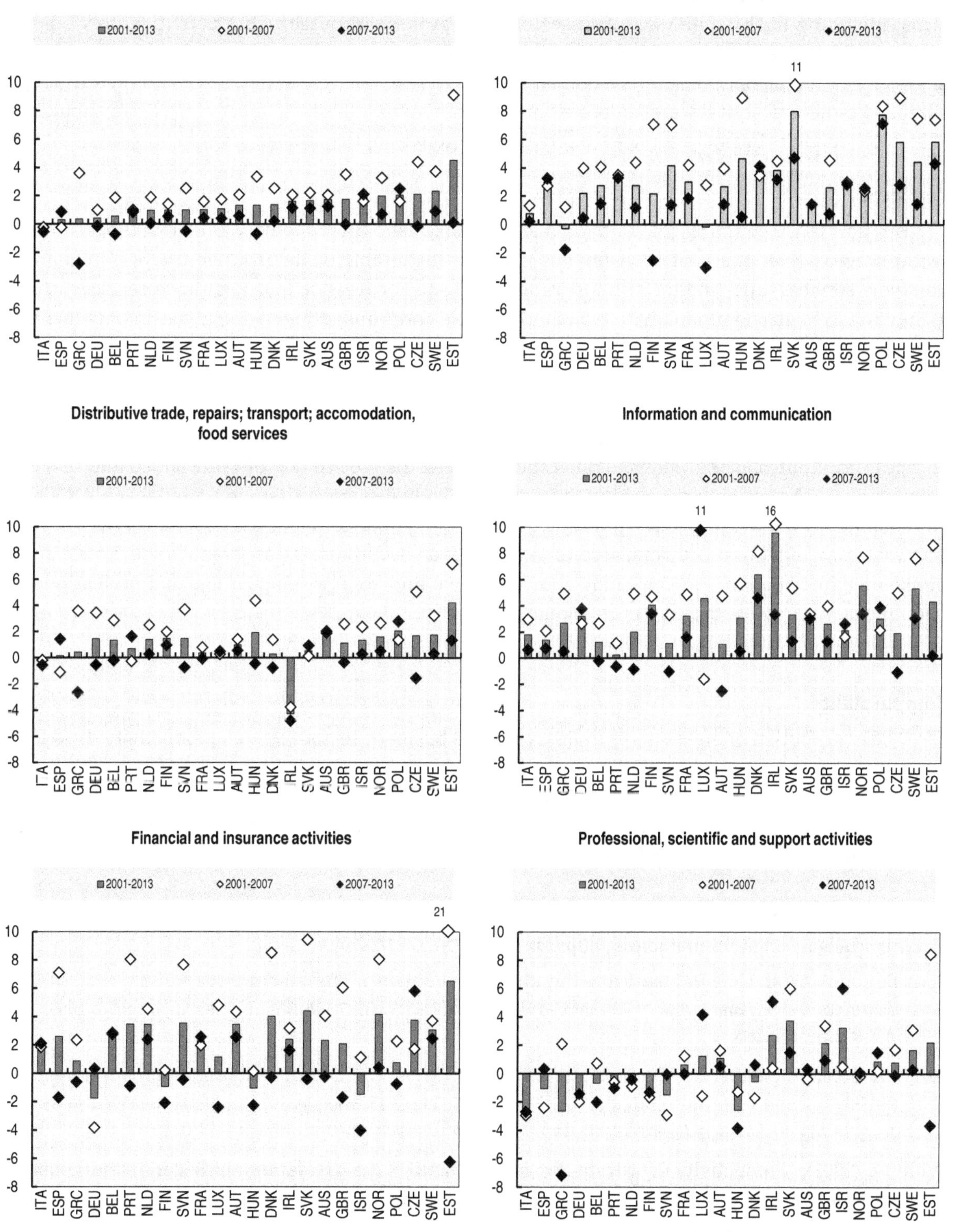

StatLink http://dx.doi.org/10.1787/888933203515

Contributions to business sector services' productivity

The business services sector has contributed significantly to GDP growth across OECD countries in recent decades, driven in large part by an increase in firms providing intermediate services to other firms, including in the manufacturing sector. This process of outsourcing activities previously conducted in-house has increased efficiencies, and hence, labour productivity, of both outsourcing firms as well as the specialised intermediary firms. Hence, over the long term, both factors may produce a structural shift towards intermediate services industries and a direct positive contribution of high productivity business services to productivity growth of the total economy.

Key facts

For most OECD countries for which data are available, labour productivity growth in the business sector services over the past 10 years was mainly attributable to distributive trade, hotels and transport services, and finance and insurance services. For finance and insurance services, this mainly reflected strong productivity growth. For hotels and transport services, it was mainly due to large shares of these activities in total business sector services value added and hours worked.

Definition

The contribution of each services sector to labour productivity growth of total business sector services is computed as the weighted difference between the growth rate of value added and that of hours worked. The weights are computed as each individual sector's share in nominal value added and total hours worked respectively of total business sector services. Business sector services cover wholesale and retail trade, repairs, accommodation, food and transport services ("trade, hotels and transport"); information and communication; financial and insurance activities; and professional, scientific and support activities ("professional services").

Information on data for Israel: *http://dx.doi.org/10.1787/888932315602*.

Comparability

The contribution of one services industry to total business sector services productivity depends critically on its share as measured by nominal value added, respectively hours worked. In addition to the difficulties encountered in measuring real value added, it is also difficult to accurately measure nominal output and value added for some services. In financial services, for example, the services provided are not always charged for explicitly and can only be measured indirectly.

Sources and further reading

OECD Productivity Statistics (database), *http://dx.doi.org/10.1787/pdtvy-data-en*.

Pilat, D. and A. Wölfl (2005), "Measuring the Interaction between Manufacturing and Services", *OECD Science, Technology and Industry Working Papers*, No. 2005/05, OECD Publishing, Paris, *http://dx.doi.org/10.1787/882376471514*.

Wölfl, A. (2005), "The Service Economy in OECD Countries: OECD/Centre d'études prospectives et d'informations internationales (CEPII)", *OECD Science, Technology and Industry Working Papers*, No. 2005/03, *http://dx.doi.org/10.1787/212257000720*.

Wölfl, A. (2003), "Productivity Growth in Services Industries: An Assessment of Recent Patterns and the Role of Measurement", *OECD Science, Technology and Industry Working Papers*, No. 2003/07, OECD Publishing, Paris, *http://dx.doi.org/10.1787/086461104618*.

Figure 2.4. **Contributions to productivity growth of business sector services**

Real value added per hour worked, percentage point contribution at annual rate

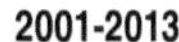

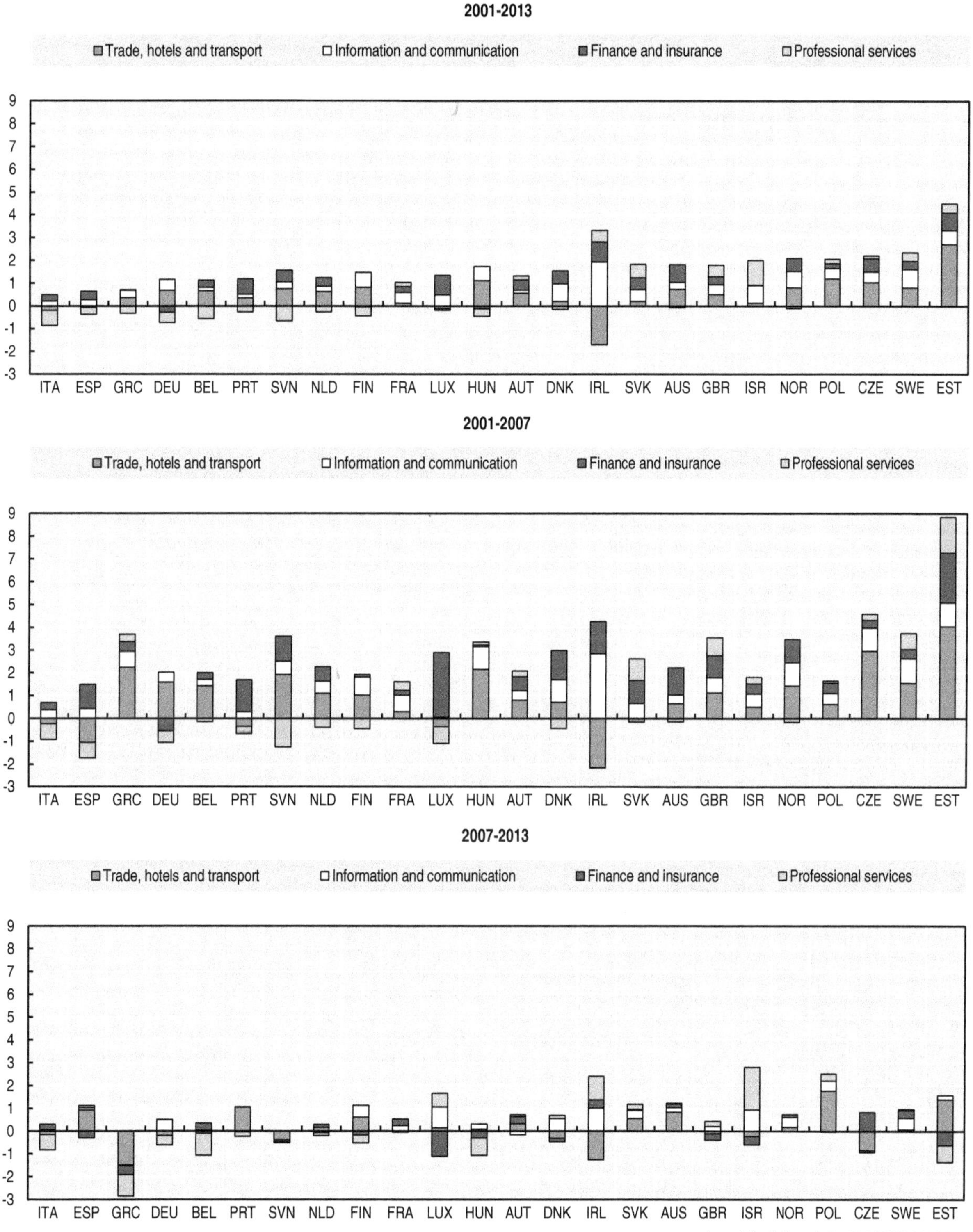
2001-2013
Trade, hotels and transport
Information and communication
Finance and insurance
Professional services
9 8 7 6 5 4 3 2 1 0 -1 -2 -3
ITA ESP GRC DEU BEL PRT SVN NLD FIN FRA LUX HUN AUT DNK IRL SVK AUS GBR ISR NOR POL CZE SWE EST
2001-2007
Trade, hotels and transport
Information and communication
Finance and insurance
Professional services
9 8 7 6 5 4 3 2 1 0 -1 -2 -3
ITA ESP GRC DEU BEL PRT SVN NLD FIN FRA LUX HUN AUT DNK IRL SVK AUS GBR ISR NOR POL CZE SWE EST
2007-2013
Trade, hotels and transport
Information and communication
Finance and insurance
Professional services
9 8 7 6 5 4 3 2 1 0 -1 -2 -3
ITA ESP GRC DEU BEL PRT SVN NLD FIN FRA LUX HUN AUT DNK IRL SVK AUS GBR ISR NOR POL CZE SWE EST

StatLink http://dx.doi.org/10.1787/888933203523

Chapter 3

Productivity, trade and international competitiveness

Unit labour costs

International competitiveness

Trade and productivity

Unit labour costs

Unit labour costs (ULC) reflect total labour costs relative to a volume of output. Hence, the growth in unit labour costs is often viewed as a broad measure of (international) price competitiveness of firms within a country.

Key facts

Over the last ten years, firms in the G7 countries and most of the early members of the euro area increased their competitiveness relative to those of other countries. Very low increases in ULC have typically been achieved by keeping unit labour costs low in both manufacturing and business sector services, as was the case in Austria, Germany and Sweden.

Within Europe, Ireland, Spain, Portugal and Greece, saw strong falls in their ULC since the onset of the financial crisis. However, care is needed in interpreting these results as improved relative competiveness, as they need to be balanced against the significant falls in output and labour input seen during that period. In Germany, improvements in competitiveness during the first half of the 2000s show signs of being reversed in the second half of the 2000s.

Comparing the data for ULC with those for labour productivity growth provides information on the possible sources for changes in ULC. For instance, over the past 10 years, some countries, notably those countries with relatively low growth in ULC, such as Austria, Germany, Israel, Poland, and Sweden, displayed stronger or equal growth in labour productivity than in ULCs. In these countries, relatively higher productivity growth coincided with wage moderation. In contrast, in most of those countries where a relative deterioration in competitiveness could be observed, there was also relatively weak growth in labour productivity.

Definition

ULCs are defined as the average cost of labour per unit of output produced. They can be expressed as the ratio of total labour compensation per hour worked to output per hour worked (labour productivity). Compensation of employees is defined as the total remuneration payable by an enterprise to an employee in return for work done by the latter during the accounting period. It includes wages and salaries payable in cash or in kind, as well as social insurance contributions paid by employers. Total labour compensation is for total persons employed and so includes employees and the self-employed.

Information on data for Israel: *http://dx.doi.org/10.1787/888932315602*.

Comparability

The data are presented for the total economy, manufacturing and business sector services (which exclude real estate activities) according to the ISIC Rev. 4 classification. All the ULC components are sourced from the *OECD National Accounts Statistics* (database), and ULCs are disseminated in the *OECD Productivity Statistics* (database). The figures present the data for those countries for which time series of sectoral hours worked are available in the *OECD National Accounts Statistics* (database).

Manufacturing ULCs are often perceived as more representative for assessing competition in tradable products. Services prices are often not very reliable, which may affect the cross-country comparability of measured business sector services ULC.

Sources and further reading

OECD *Main Economic Indicators* (database), *http://dx.doi.org/10.1787/mei-data-en*.

OECD National Accounts Statistics (database), *http://dx.doi.org/10.1787/na-data-en*.

OECD Productivity Statistics (database), *http://dx.doi.org/10.1787/pdtvy-data-en*.

Figure 3.1. **Unit labour costs, hourly labour compensation and productivity, total economy**

Percentage change at annual rate

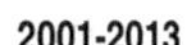

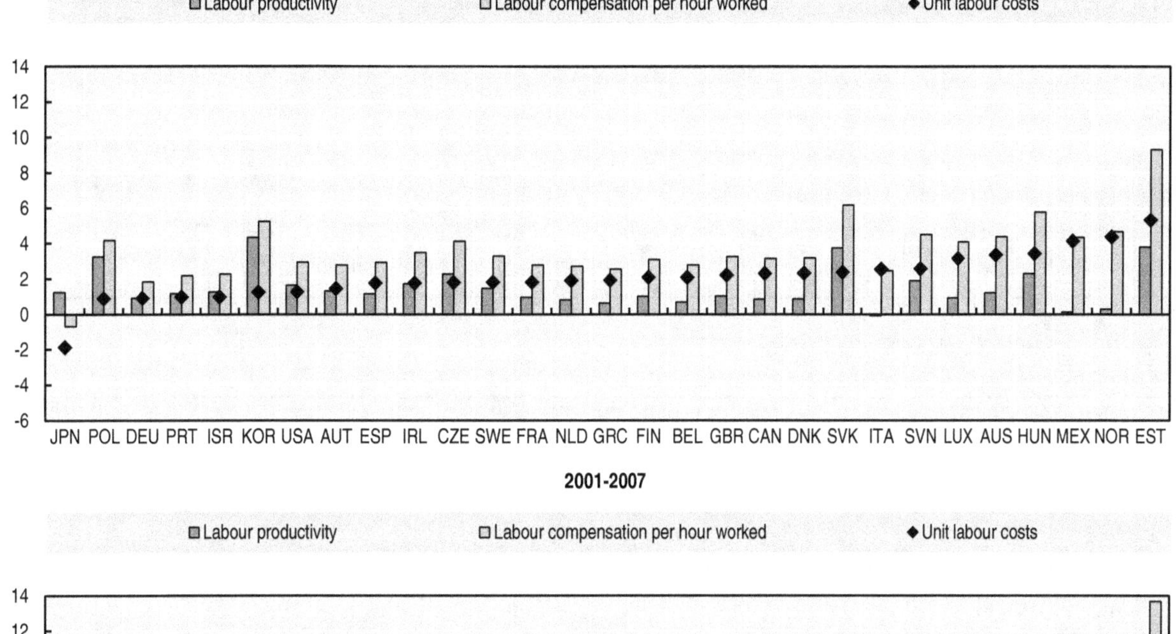

2001-2007

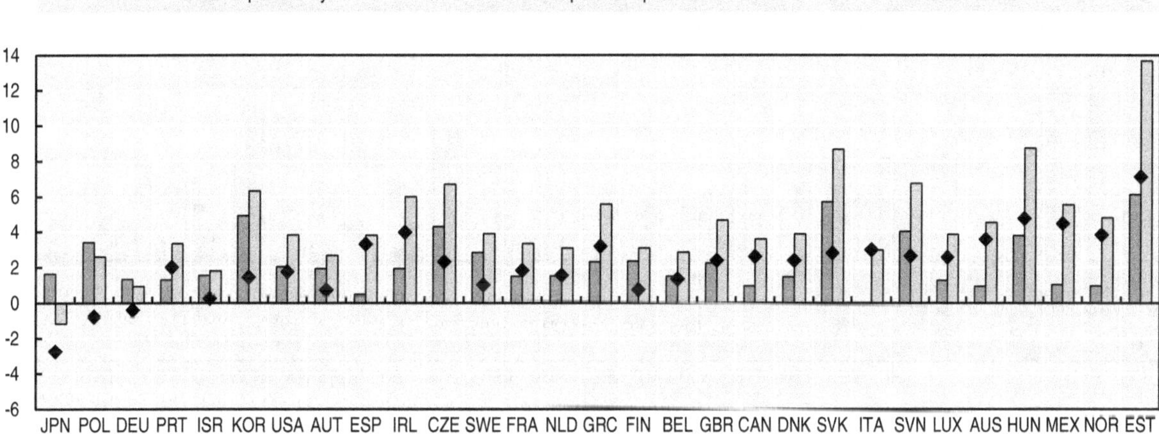

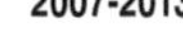

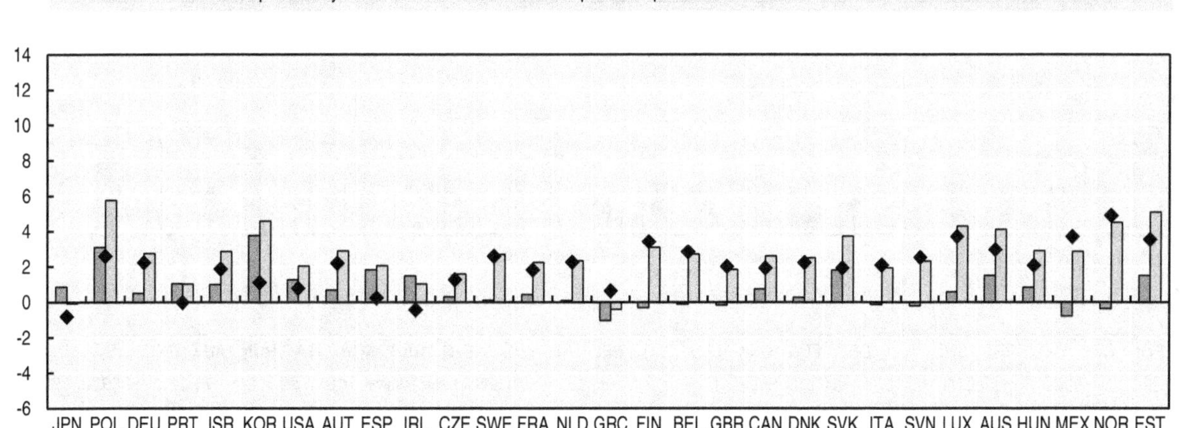

StatLink http://dx.doi.org/10.1787/888933203535

Figure 3.2. **Unit labour costs, hourly labour compensation and productivity, manufacturing**

Percentage change at annual rate

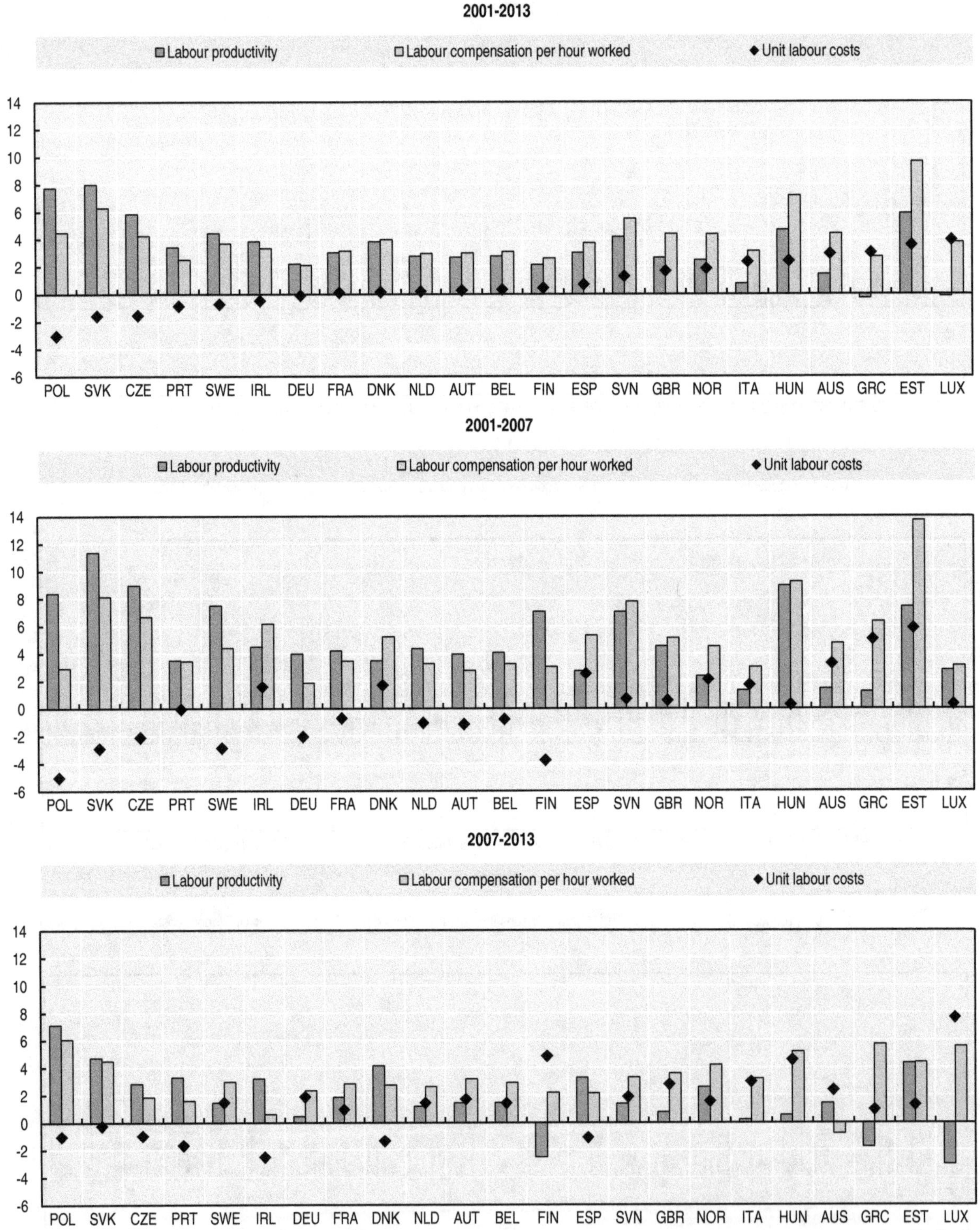

StatLink http://dx.doi.org/10.1787/888933203543

Figure 3.3. **Unit labour costs, hourly labour compensation and productivity, business sector services**

Percentage change at annual rate

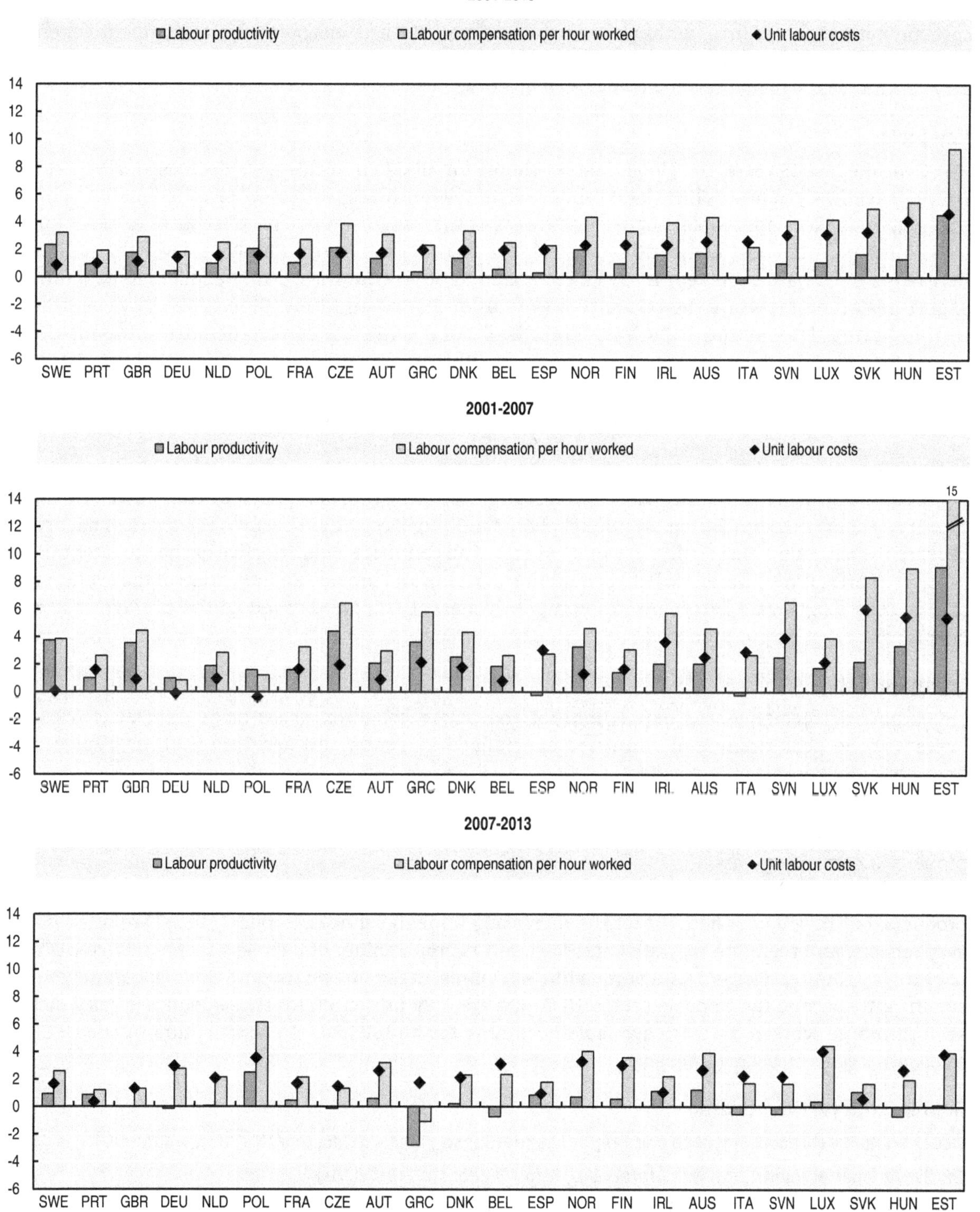

StatLink http://dx.doi.org/10.1787/888933203555

International competitiveness

Despite their frequent use, unit labour costs (ULC) are an incomplete measure of international competitiveness and they need to be complemented with other indicators. In an era of global value chains, a measure based only on the costs of domestic labour may not be representative of overall cost competitiveness of firms within a country. Moreover, ULC as a measure of price-competitiveness cannot capture the capacity of firms to serve international markets through high quality goods and services and where demand is relatively price inelastic.

Key facts

Over the last 15 years, the global market shares for all G7 countries have decreased, albeit at a slower pace in Germany, which kept labour costs low with respect to other G7 countries. This observation is more noticeable for the euro area countries which do not have recourse to exchange rate adjustment to boost competitiveness relative to other euro area countries. Over the period, Germany's ULCs have been kept in check compared to other countries, partly explaining its strong export performance, while the opposite was true for France and Italy. Since 2009, however, the United States, France and Italy have stabilised their export performance and indeed, the United States' global market share has picked up, although remaining at significantly lower levels than in the beginning of the 2000s. For the United Kingdom, despite a declining real effective exchange rate over the last 15 years, the global market share decreased.

Definition

Export performance is measured as actual growth in exports relative to the growth of the country's export market. The export market share for a single country measures the share of exports by firms in that country in relation to world exports of all countries. Real effective exchange rates take account of price level differences between trading partners and provide an indication of the evolution of a country's aggregate external price competitiveness. ULCs are defined as the average cost of labour per unit of output produced.

Comparability

Export performance and export market shares are based on gross trade data which may overstate the performance of countries specialised in goods and services that are typically downstream in global value-chains.

Trade statistics do not always consistently measure flows between affiliated enterprises. This is especially so for trade in intellectual property products where payments may often be recorded as property income payments.

Manufacturing ULCs are often perceived as more representative for competition in tradable products, but they do not account for the increasing trade in services. Services prices are often not very reliable, and therefore may affect cross-country comparability of business sector service ULCs. Looking at total economy ULCs somewhat alleviates these concerns, but their coverage goes significantly beyond the tradable sector. ULC data are only presented for those countries for which sectoral hours worked data are available according to the ISIC Rev. 4 classification in the OECD *National Accounts Statistics* (database).

Sources and further reading

OECD Economic Outlook: Statistics and Projections (database), *http://dx.doi.org/10.1787/eo-data-en*.

OECD National Accounts Statistics (database), *http://dx.doi.org/10.1787/na-data-en*.

OECD Productivity Statistics (database), *http://dx.doi.org/10.1787/pdtvy-data-en*.

Durand, M., J. Simon and C. Webb (1992), "OECD's Indicators of International Trade and Competitiveness", *OECD Economics Department Working Papers*, No. 120, OECD Publishing, Paris, *http://dx.doi.org/10.1787/708306180711*.

Figure 3.4. **Indicators of international competitiveness**

Indices, 1999 = 100

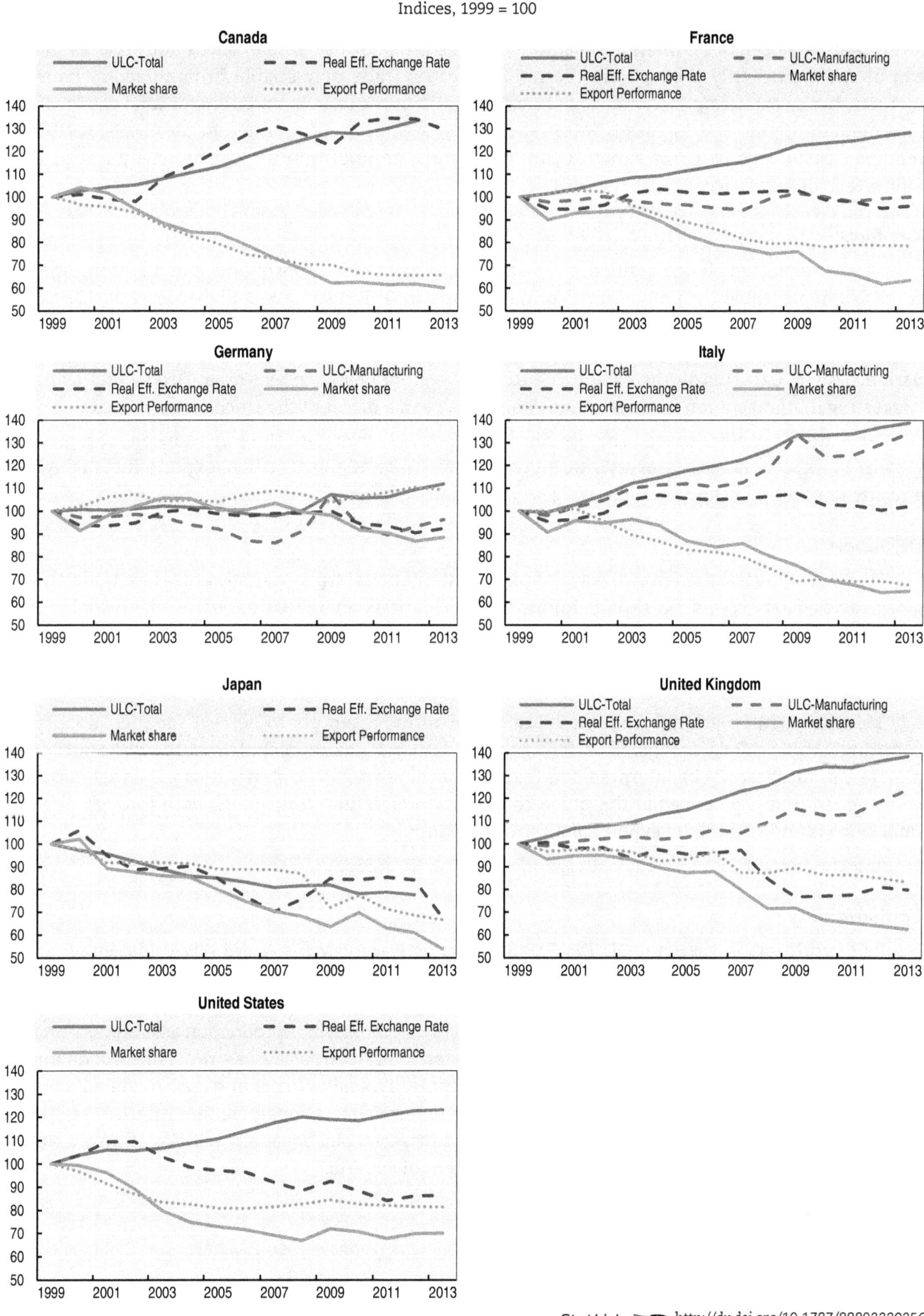

StatLink http://dx.doi.org/10.1787/888933203568

Trade and productivity

Economic theory suggests that more open countries should grow faster and have higher income levels than less open ones. International trade enables firms to specialise in goods and services that can be most efficiently produced in the home country. Trade may enable firms to sell to larger markets, hence exploiting economies of scale. Trade also puts pressure on prices for final goods and intermediate inputs and increases international fragmentation of production processes, further reducing costs. Finally, firms exposed to international competition are continuously forced to innovate in order to succeed.

Key facts

The empirical evidence confirms the strong link between exports and growth. More open countries, represented by a higher ratio of net exports to GDP, also have a higher level of GDP per capita as compared to countries with lower net exports. Moreover, countries that have been able to increase their export-to-GDP ratio over time have also improved labour productivity over the same period. This is particularly the case for "catch-up" economies such as Korea, Turkey and Chile, suggesting that integration in global value chains has been a driver of the catching up process.

Measures of exports based on gross terms can however overstate the importance that a given growth in exports makes to overall GDP growth; this reflects the fact that exports increasingly embody imports.

Definition

Trade can be measured in two ways. Typically international trade statistics measure trade on a gross basis as net exports, i.e. exports minus imports. Exports on a gross basis include the value of imports embodied in goods and services as well as some value-added created in other domestic sectors that returns embodied in imports. This "double-counting" particularly affects those countries where firms are closely integrated into global value chains.

Measuring international trade in value-added terms attempts to correct for this "double-counting". Value-added embodied in foreign final demand – as represented in the bottom right panel – can most readily be interpreted as "exports of value-added". It shows how industries export value added that is produced in the home country to foreign final consumers, both through direct final exports and via indirect exports of intermediate inputs.

Information on data for Israel: *http://dx.doi.org/10.1787/888932315602*.

Comparability

The indicators in the joint *OECD/WTO: Statistics on Trade in Value Added (TiVA)* (database) are derived from OECD Input Output Tables linked together using bilateral trade flows in goods and services. Some assumptions are necessary to create the TiVA indicators, implying that some care is needed in interpreting the results. Key in this context is the underlying "production assumption" that assumes that for a given industry, all firms allocated to that industry use the same goods and services, and so imports, to produce the same outputs. Typically, firms engaged in global value chains, particularly foreign owned affiliates, are likely to have higher import content than firms in the same sector producing goods or services for domestic markets. This means that TiVA estimates will, more likely than not, underestimate the import content of exports.

Sources and further reading

OECD National Accounts Statistics (database), *http://dx.doi.org/10.1787/na-data-en*.

OECD/WTO: Statistics on Trade in Value Added (TiVA) (database), *http://dx.doi.org/10.1787/data-00648-en*.

OECD-WTO (2012), *Trade in Value-Added: Concepts, Methodologies and Challenges (Joint OECD-WTO Note)*, OECD, Paris, *www.oecd.org/sti/ind/49894138.pdf*.

Figure 3.5. **Net exports to GDP ratio and GDP per capita *vis-à-vis* the OECD, 2013**

Total economy, in %, OECD = 100

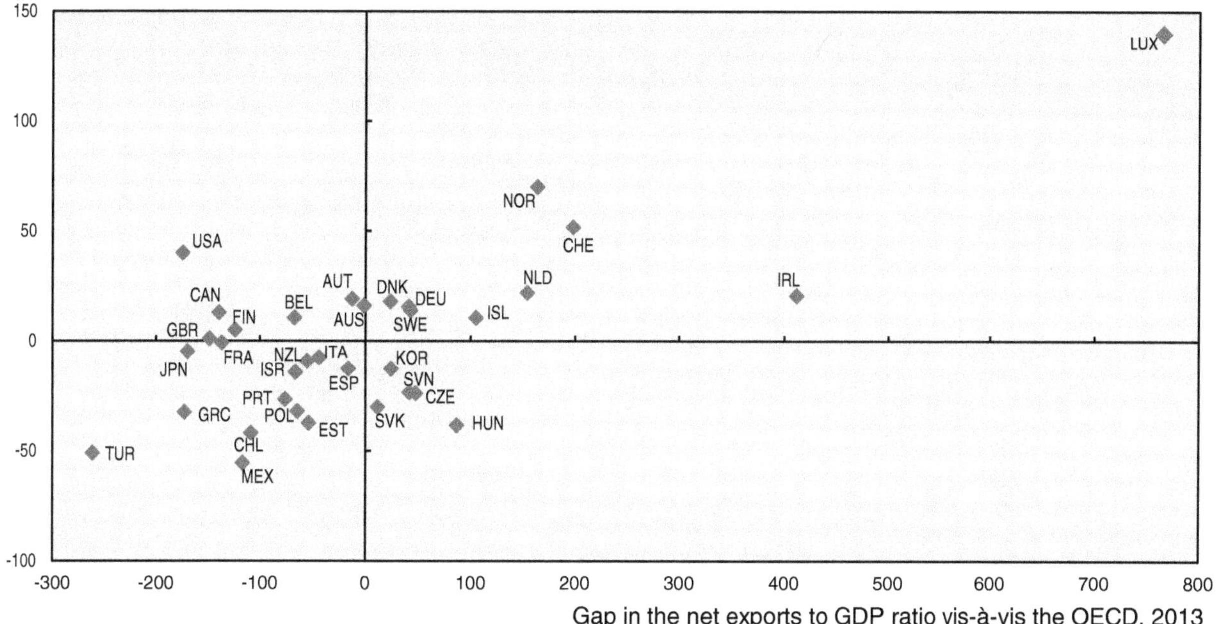

StatLink http://dx.doi.org/10.1787/888933203576

Figure 3.6. **Change in exports to GDP ratio and growth in GDP per hour worked**

Total economy, exports in gross terms (left panel) and in value added terms (right panel)

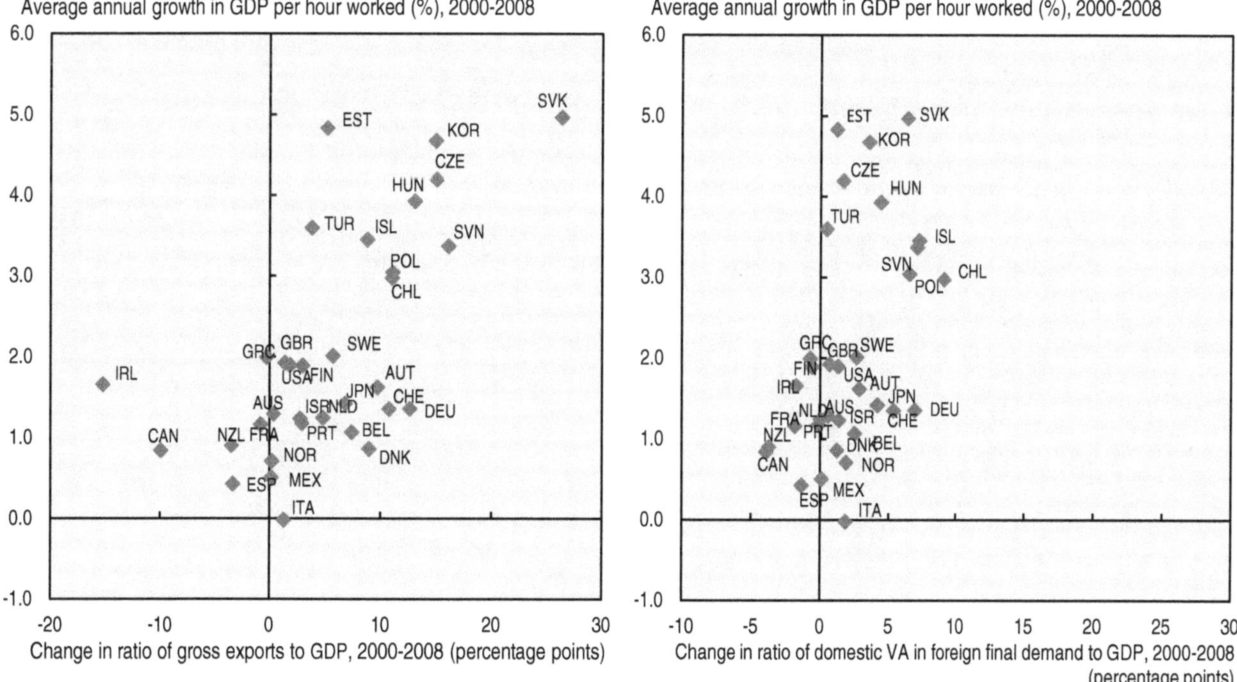

StatLink http://dx.doi.org/10.1787/888933203585

Chapter 4

Productivity trends

Trends in labour productivity growth

Trends in components of labour productivity growth

Multifactor productivity over the cycle

Trends in labour productivity growth

Labour productivity is a key driver of economic growth and living standards. Understanding how much actual labour productivity growth is driven by structural factors and how much by reactions to the productivity cycle or the economic cycle is hence important for policy makers. This requires decomposing the time series of actual annual labour productivity growth into a trend (or structural) component and a cyclical component.

Key facts

Looked over the last three decades, labour productivity growth has followed different trends across the G7 countries. But seen over the 10 years preceding the crisis, trend labour productivity growth has declined for nearly all G7 countries, the fall being particularly marked in France, Italy and Japan. In the case of the Canada, the United Kingdom and the United States, the decline since the end-1990s marked some reversal of a previous acceleration. In the other countries, trend labour productivity growth has shown a gradual decline almost throughout the past 30 years, and in the case of Japan, from relatively high rates.

While one needs to be cautious in interpreting this as a post-crisis trend, especially in view of the volatility introduced by the crisis, average labour productivity growth over the 2007-13 period declined significantly in France and the United Kingdom. Average productivity growth over the same period also fell in Japan and the United States but at a more moderate rate.*

Definition

Labour productivity is defined as GDP per hour worked and its growth rate is calculated as its first natural-log difference. The decomposition of labour productivity growth into a trend and a cyclical component is done by applying the Hodrick-Prescott (HP) filter (Hodrick and Prescott, 1997), where the trend component is meant to capture the long-term growth of the series and the cyclical component is the deviation from that trend. In the HP filter, the smoothness of the trend depends on a parameter usually identified as λ. The larger the value given to λ, the smoother is the trend.

Comparability

Like other filters, one limitation of the HP filter is that the estimated trend is more sensitive to transitory shocks or short-term fluctuations at the end of the sample period. This results in a sub-optimal performance of the HP filter at the endpoints of the series (Baxter and King, 1999). In view of this property, trend series are not published for the last two years for which data on actual labour productivity growth are available.

An important aspect of the HP filter is the value of the smoothing parameter λ. While for quarterly data it has been typically assumed a value of $\lambda = 1\,600$ (as recommended by Hodrick and Prescott, 1997), there is less agreement on the value to be used when the filter is applied to other frequencies (e.g. annual, monthly). The value of λ selected here has been determined by calibrating the Hodrick-Prescott filter in such a way that cycles shorter than 9.5 years are attenuated by 90% or more (see Annex F).

Sources and further reading

OECD *Productivity Statistics* (database), *http://dx.doi.org/10.1787/pdtvy-data-en.*

Baxter, M. and R.G. King (1999), "Measuring Business Cycles: Approximate Band-Pass Filters for Economic Time Series", *The Review of Economics and Statistics*, Vol. 81, No. 4.

Hodrick, R.J. and E.C. Prescott (1997), "Postwar US Business Cycles: An Empirical Investigation", *Journal of Money, Credit and Banking*, Vol. 29, No. 1.

OECD (2001), *Measuring Productivity – OECD Manual: Measurement of Aggregate and Industry-level Productivity Growth*, OECD Publishing, Paris, *http://dx.doi.org/10.1787/9789264194519-en.*

* Official data for Germany after unification are available only from 1991 onwards. In order to estimate data for the whole of Germany back to 1985, the secretariat has estimated data for the whole of Germany back to 1970 by linking in 1991 the data for Germany to historical data for West Germany.

Figure 4.1. **Labour productivity growth and its trend**

Total economy, percentage change at annual rate, G7 countries

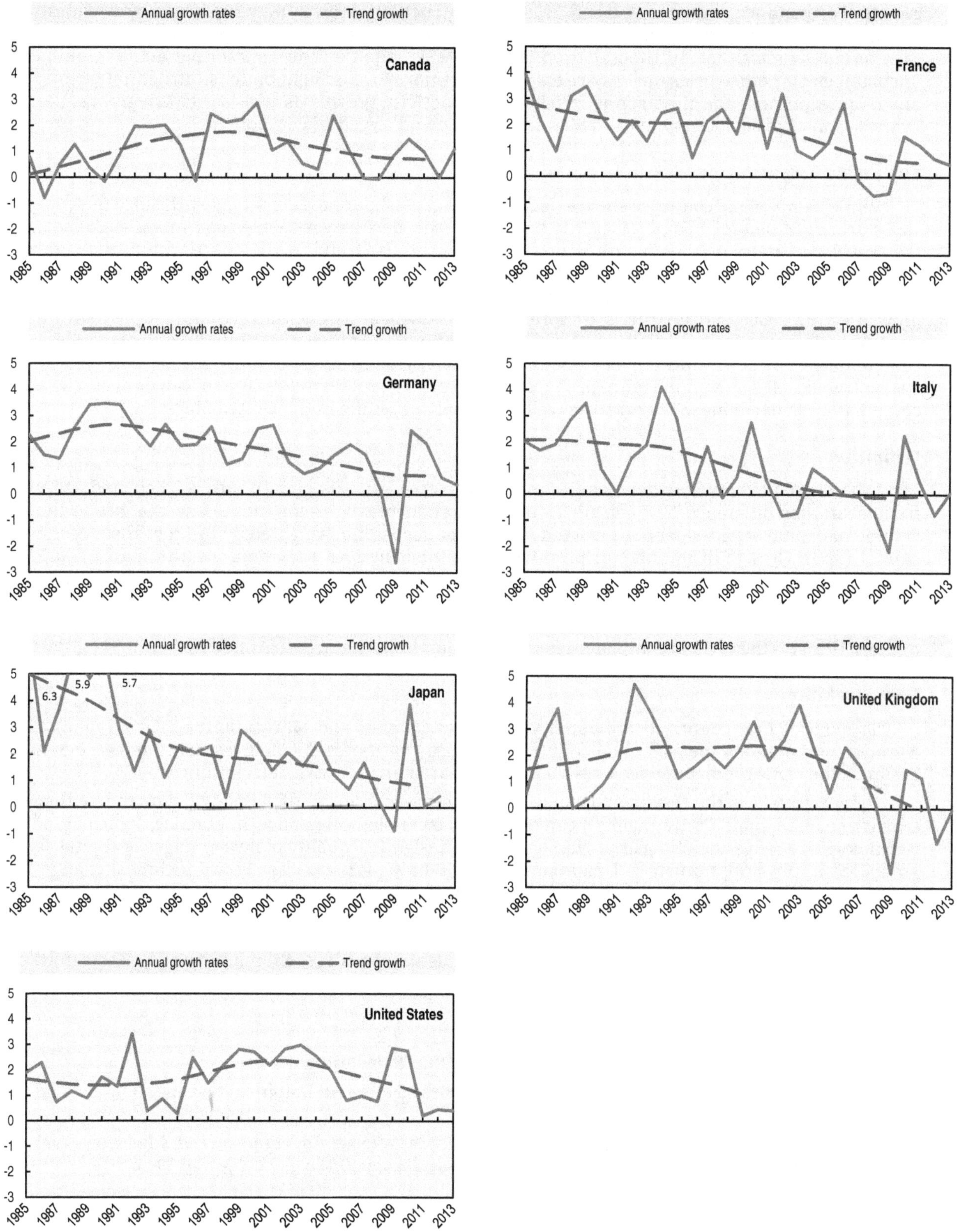

StatLink http://dx.doi.org/10.1787/888933203598

Trends in components of labour productivity growth

Policy makers are interested in analysing the structural factors determining labour productivity growth. For instance, a declining trend of labour productivity growth may be driven by declining investment in capital relative to hours worked (capital deepening). Or it could be indicative of factors that hamper growth in multifactor productivity (MFP), such as low innovative activity, skills mismatches or inefficiencies due to barriers to competition. To shed light on these structural factors, one can decompose the time series of labour productivity growth as well as its drivers, i.e. the contribution of capital deepening and MFP, into a trend and a cyclical component.

Key facts

While nearly all G7 countries show a declining trend of labour productivity growth since the end-1990s or indeed before in some cases, the sources for this decline vary across countries. In Canada, the downward trend of MFP growth contrasted with the flat trend in the contribution of capital deepening. In Germany and Italy, the trend of MFP growth has declined continuously since the beginning of the 1990s and flatted after the crisis. Japan saw a drastic decline in the trend of MFP growth in the 1980s and 1990s and a more gradual downward trend since then, coupled with a downward trend in the contribution of capital deepening. In France, the United Kingdom and the United States, the downward trend of labour productivity growth since the early 2000s was driven by a slowdown in MFP growth in France, a sharp decline in MFP growth in the United Kingdom and by a combination of declining MFP growth as well as capital deepening in the United States.*

Definition

Labour productivity is defined as GDP per hour worked and its growth rate is calculated as its first natural-log difference. The contribution of capital deepening is constructed as changes in the volume of capital services per hour worked (i.e. capital deepening) weighted by the cost share of the capital input. Growth in multifactor productivity is measured as a residual, i.e. that part of GDP growth that cannot be explained by growth in labour and capital inputs. The decomposition these series into a trend and a cyclical component is done by applying the Hodrick-Prescott (HP) filter (Hodrick and Prescott, 1997), where the trend component is meant to capture the long-term growth of the series and the cyclical component is the deviation from that trend (Annex F).

Comparability

To ensure cross-country comparability of capital services and MFP data, the OECD applies a common computation method to all countries that uses harmonised ICT investment deflators and assumes the same average service lives for any given asset irrespective of the country.

Growth in MFP is the residual part of GDP growth that cannot be explained by growth in either labour or capital input. Conceptually, it can be seen as technological change. In practice, some part of technological change, including improvements in the design and quality of new vintages of capital, is embodied in physical, notably, ICT capital. Then, MFP only picks up *disembodied* technical change, e.g. network effects or spillovers from production factors, the effects of better management practices, brand names, organisational change and general knowledge. Moreover, linked to the assumptions of the production function and data constraints hampering a precise measurement of labour and capital inputs, MFP also captures other factors, e.g. adjustment costs, economies of scale, effects from imperfect competition and measurement errors.

Sources and further reading

OECD Productivity Statistics (database), *http://dx.doi.org/10.1787/pdtvy-data-en*.

Hodrick, R.J. and E.C. Prescott (1997), "Postwar US Business Cycles: An Empirical Investigation", *Journal of Money, Credit and Banking*, Vol. 29, No. 1.

OECD (2001), *Measuring Productivity – OECD Manual: Measurement of Aggregate and Industry-level Productivity Growth*, OECD Publishing, Paris, *http://dx.doi.org/10.1787/9789264194519-en*.

* Official data for Germany after unification are available only from 1991 onwards. In order to estimate data for the whole of Germany back to 1985, the secretariat has estimated data for the whole of Germany back to 1970 by linking in 1991 the data for Germany to historical data for West Germany.

Figure 4.2. **Labour productivity growth trend and its components, Canada**

Total economy, percentage change at annual rate

Labour productivity

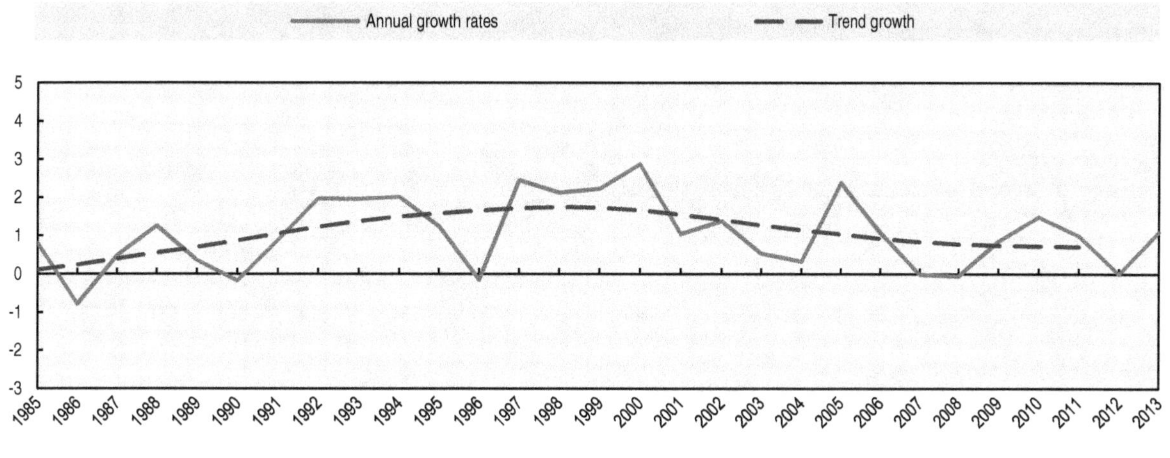

Multifactor productivity

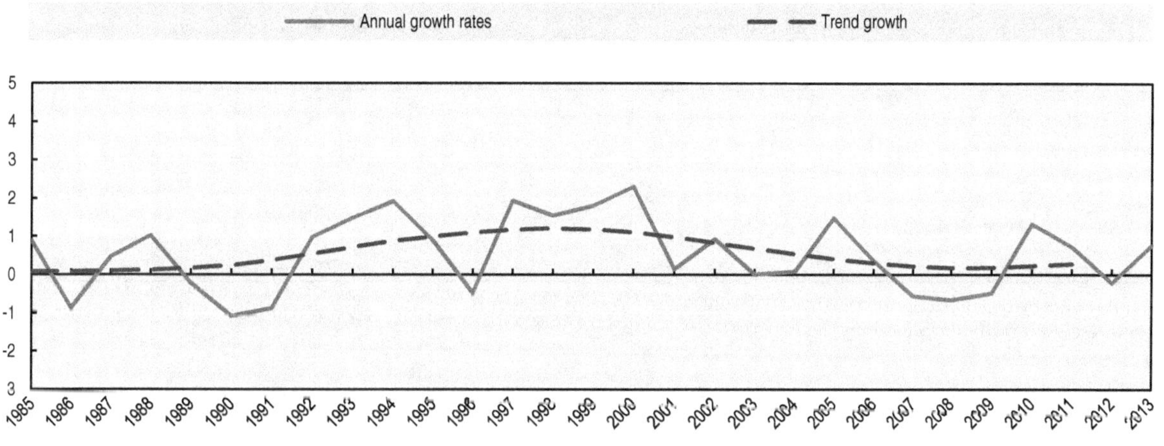

Contribution of capital deepening

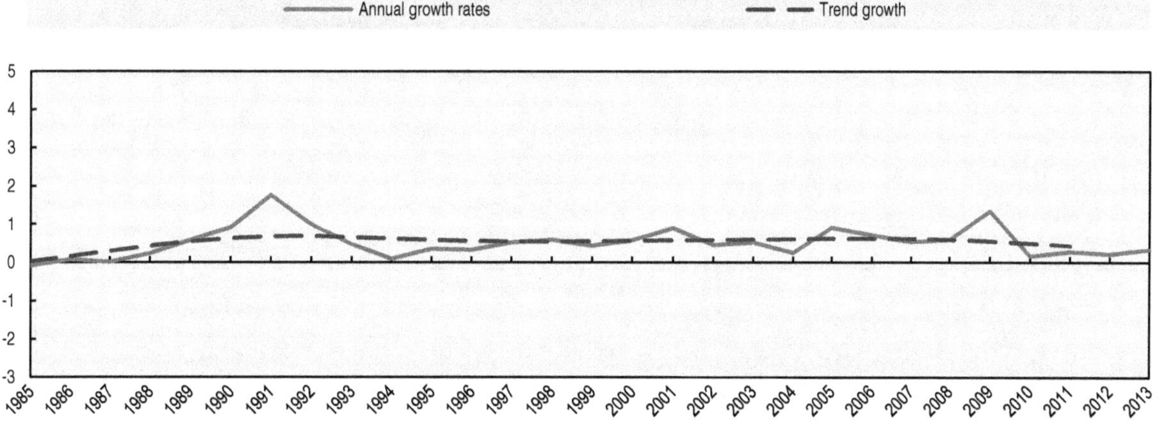

StatLink http://dx.doi.org/10.1787/888933203601

Figure 4.3. **Labour productivity growth trend and its components, France**

Total economy, percentage change at annual rate

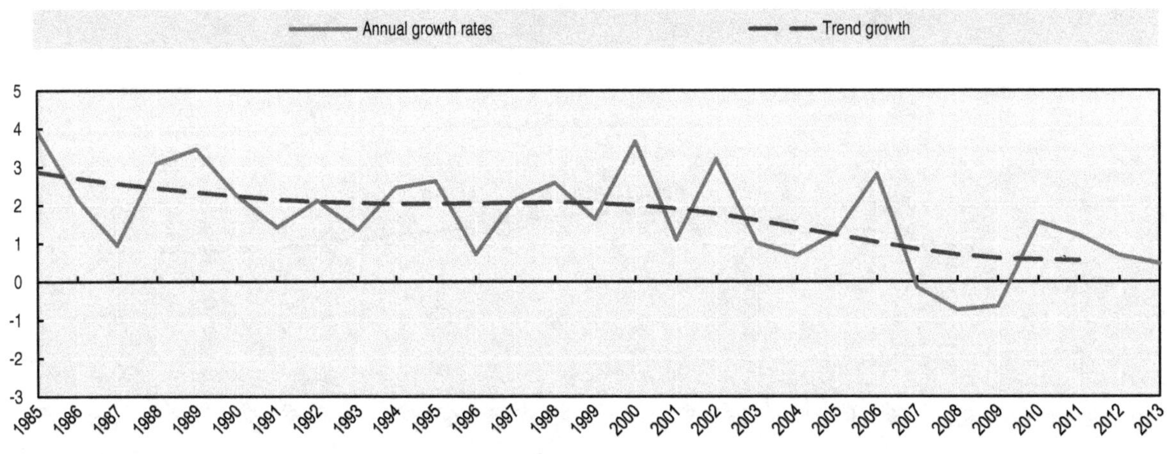

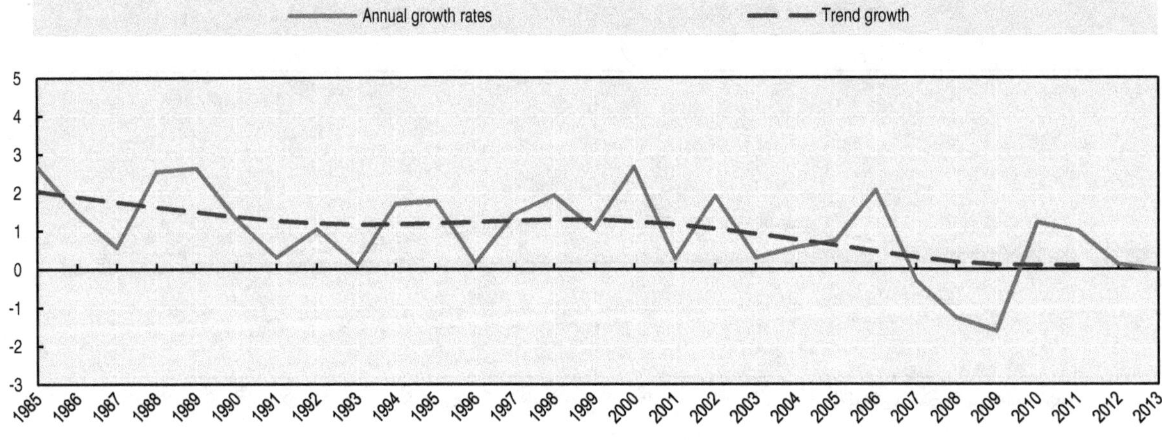

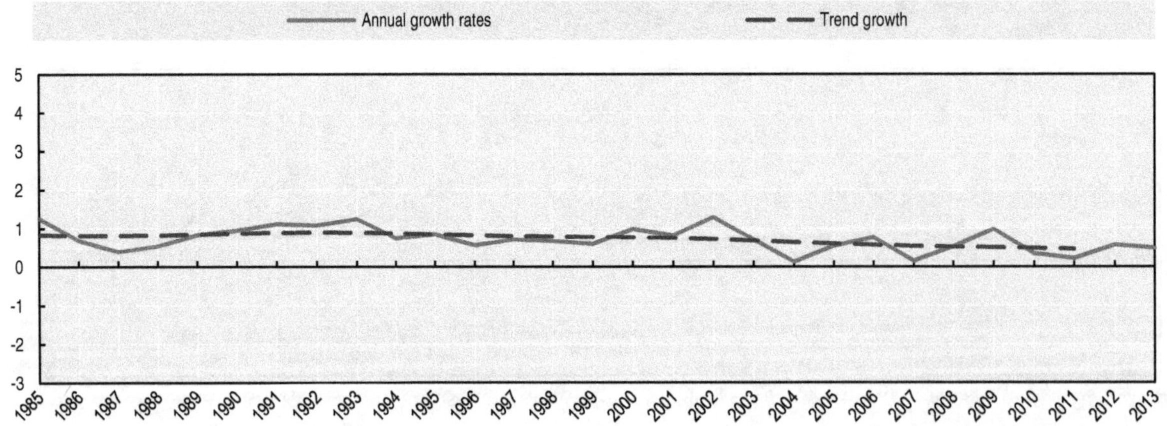

StatLink http://dx.doi.org/10.1787/888933203618

Figure 4.4. **Labour productivity growth trend and its components, Germany**

Total economy, percentage change at annual rate

Labour productivity

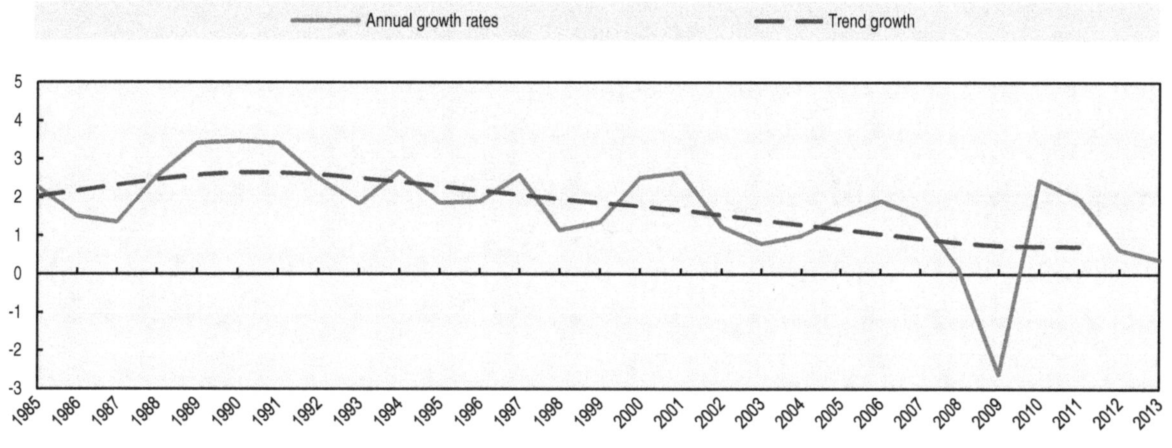

Multifactor productivity

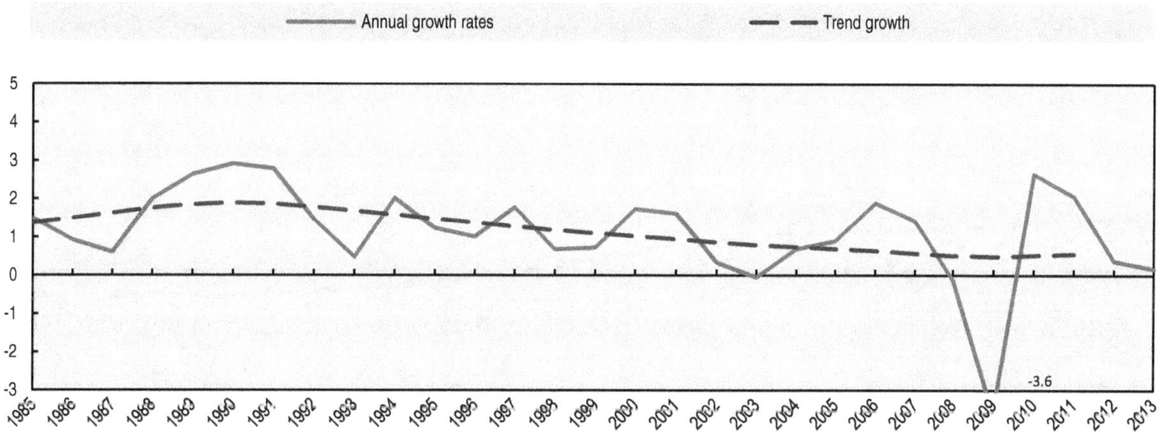

Contribution of capital deepening

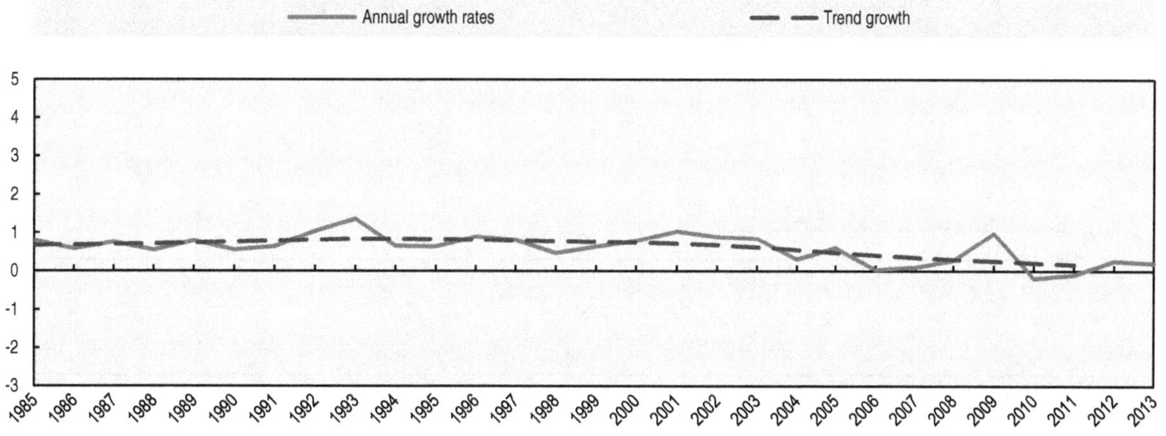

StatLink http://dx.doi.org/10.1787/888933203621

Figure 4.5. Labour productivity growth trend and its components, Italy

Total economy, percentage change at annual rate

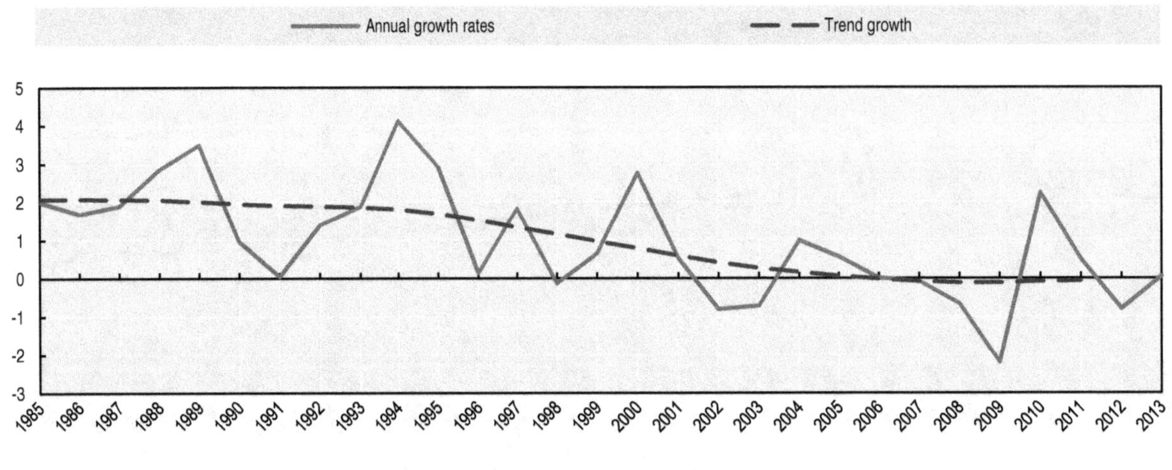

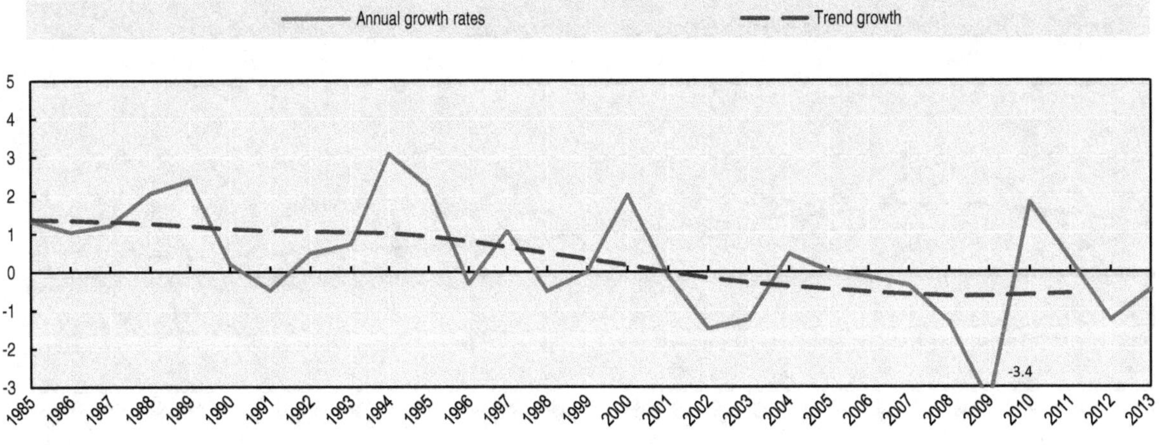

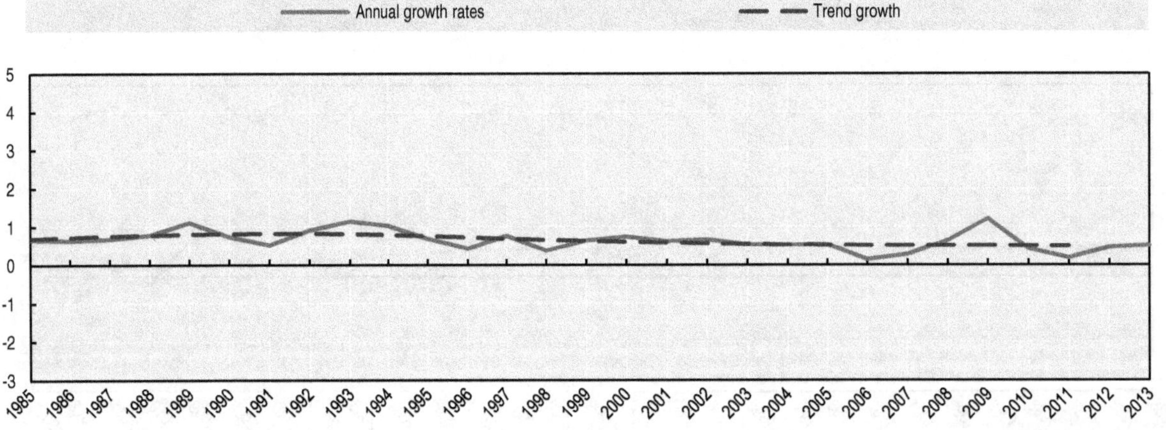

StatLink http://dx.doi.org/10.1787/888933203637

Figure 4.6. **Labour productivity growth trend and its components, Japan**

Total economy, percentage change at annual rate

Labour productivity

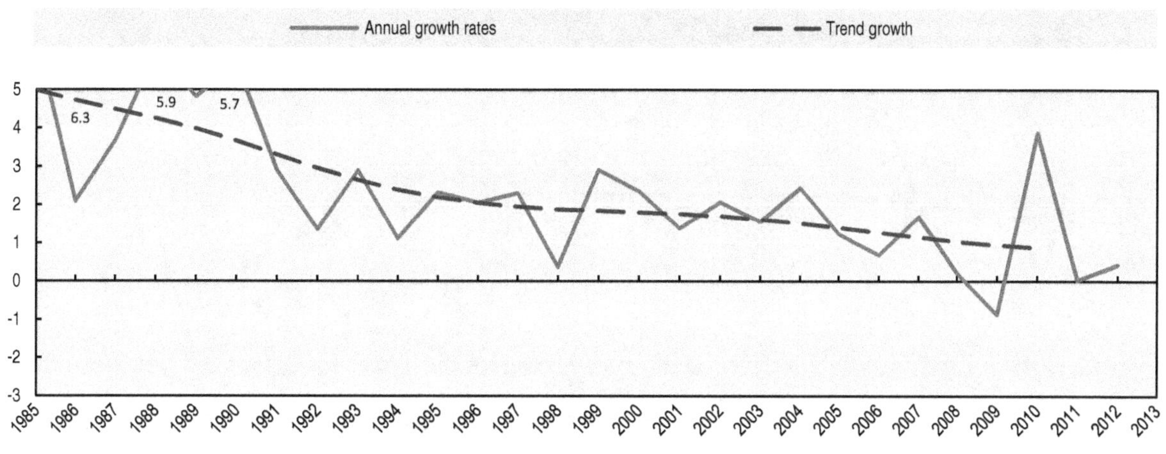

Multifactor productivity

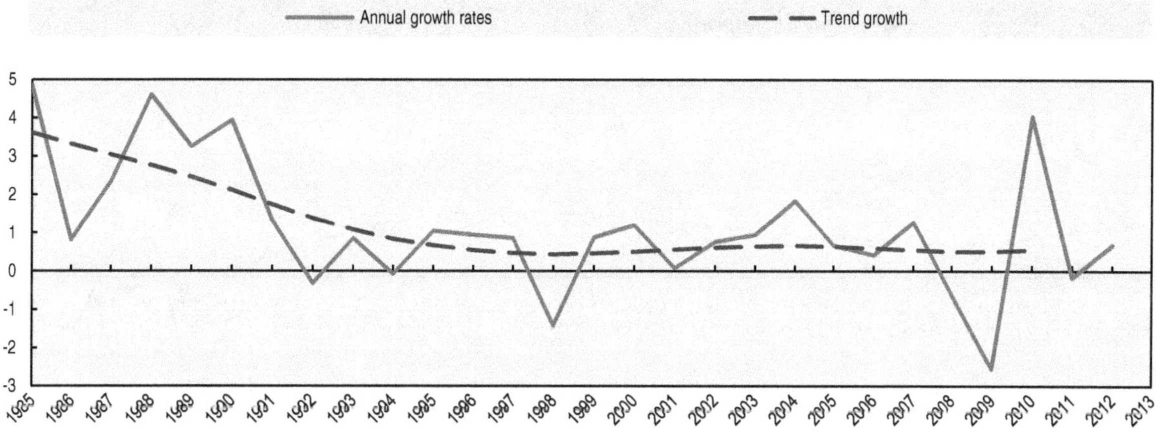

Contribution of capital deepening

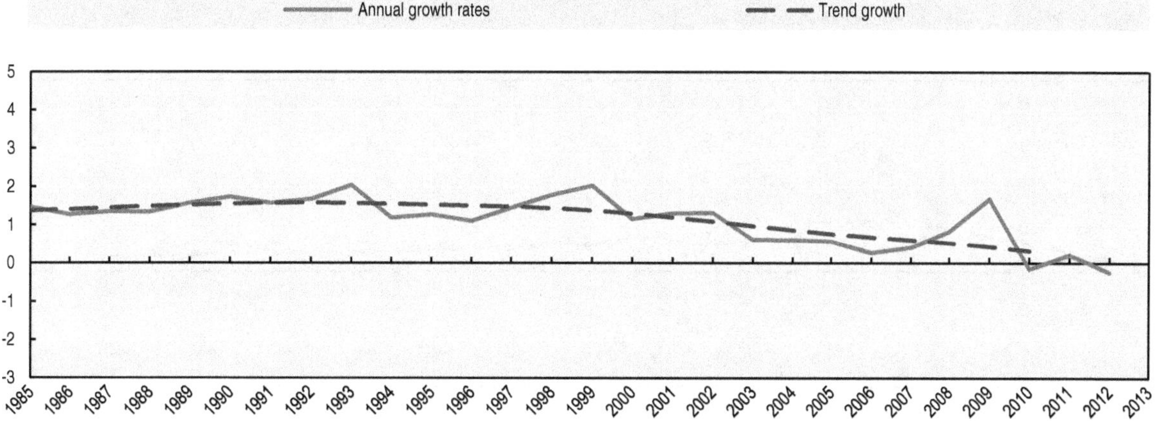

StatLink http://dx.doi.org/10.1787/888933203648

Figure 4.7. **Labour productivity growth trend and its components, United Kingdom**

Total economy, percentage change at annual rate

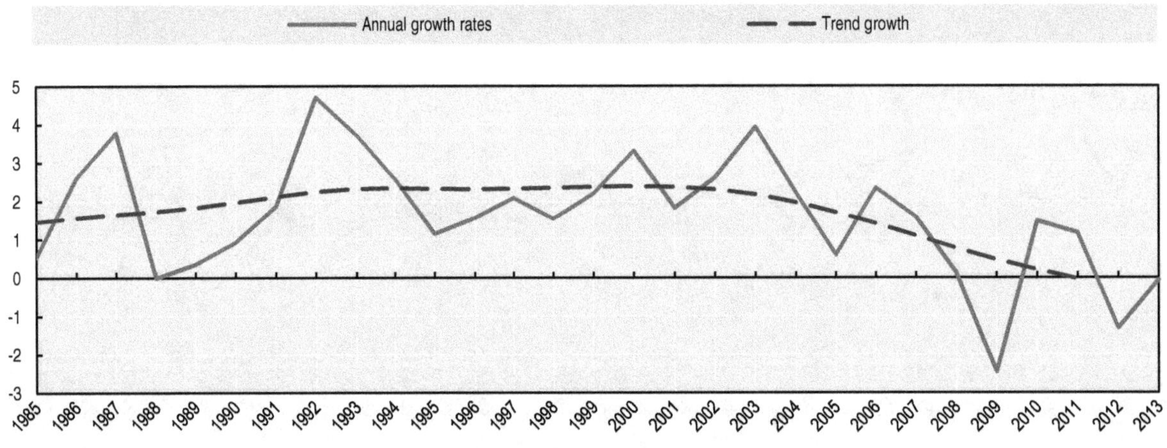

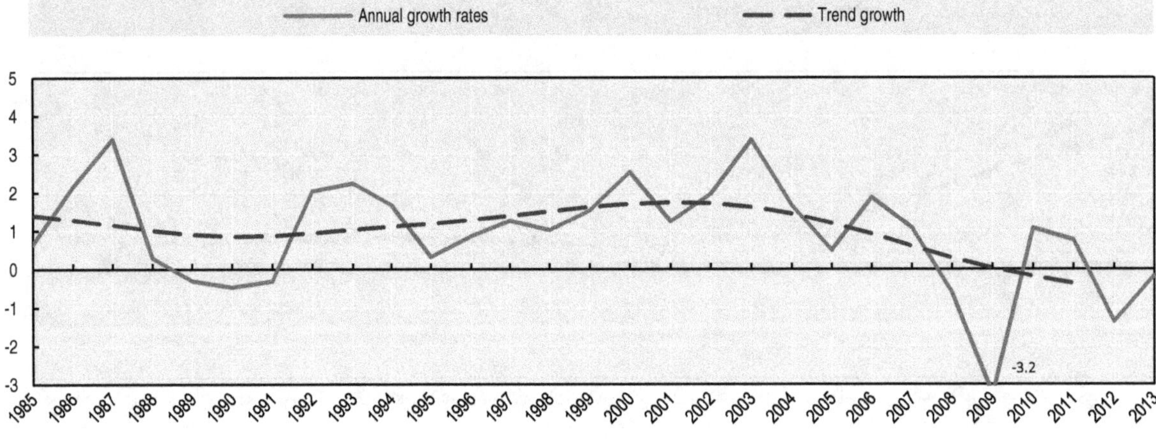

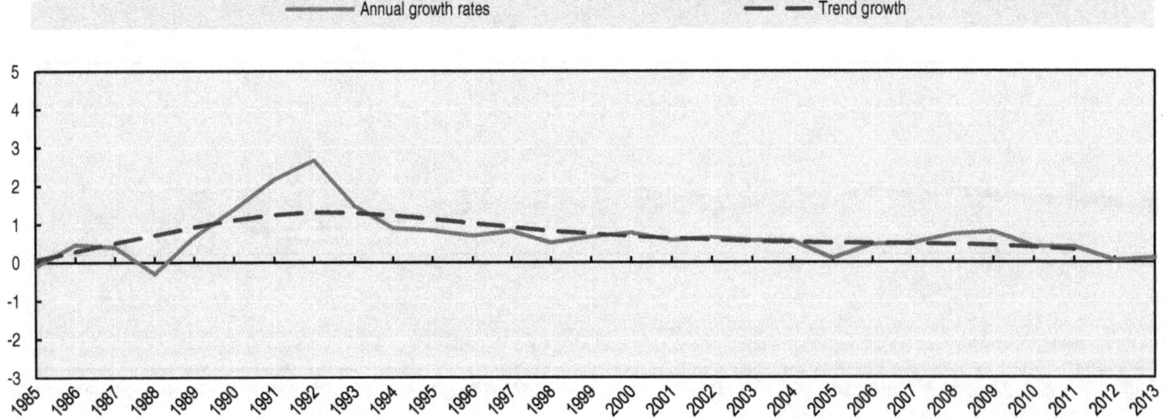

StatLink http://dx.doi.org/10.1787/888933203653

Figure 4.8. **Labour productivity growth trend and its components, United States**

Total economy, percentage change at annual rate

Labour productivity

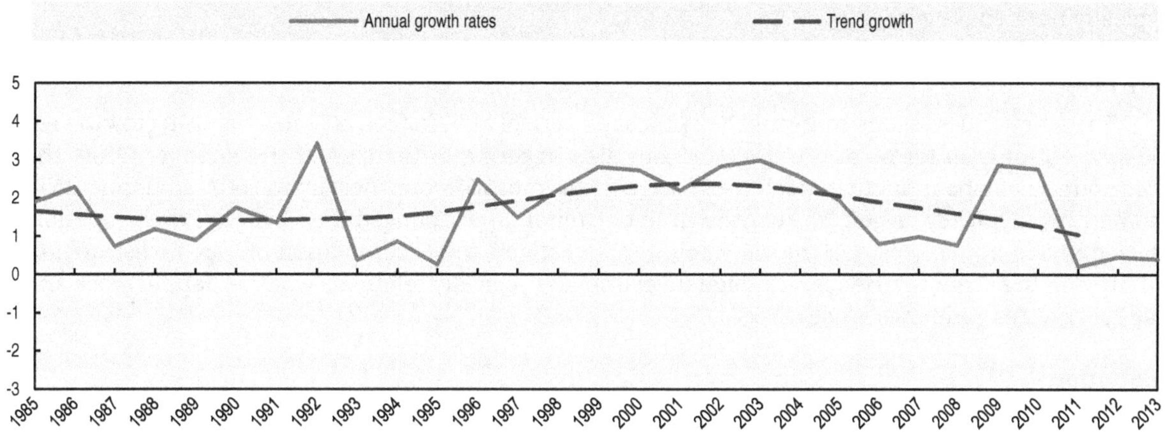

Multifactor productivity

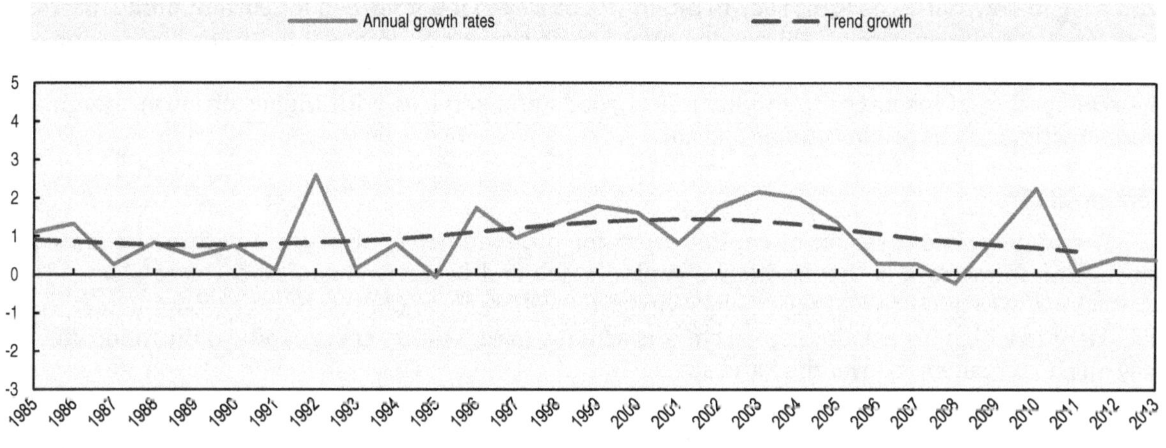

Contribution of capital deepening

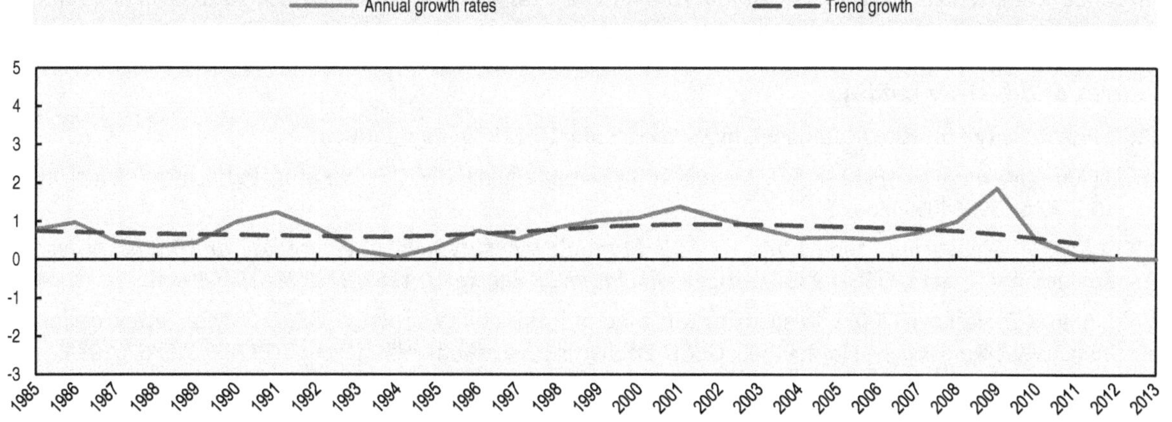

StatLink http://dx.doi.org/10.1787/888933203663

Multifactor productivity over the cycle

A number of studies indicate that multifactor productivity growth (MFP) behaves cyclically, i.e. it increases in an upturn and declines in a downturn. This has sometimes been interpreted as a paradox, as MFP has traditionally been perceived as exogenous technological change, which should typically not behave cyclically.

Key facts

The empirical evidence confirms the cyclical pattern of MFP. In fact, MFP follows GDP growth very closely, not only in terms of the direction but also in terms of the size of the change. While the contribution of labour fluctuated relatively strongly for most G7 countries, up to 2007, adjustments in labour input typically lagged. The contribution of capital input changed little over the cycle, possibly reflecting adjustment costs. Moreover, capital input reflects the accumulation of past investment of all firms in the economy. Hence, although investment is typically relatively volatile, capital stock and capital services estimates are less so.*

Definition

Four factors help explain this cyclical movement and each of them is related to the definition of MFP as the part of GDP growth that cannot be explained by changes in labour and capital inputs (Annex A). First, cycles in productivity growth may relate to imperfect competition and the potential to capitalise on increasing returns to scale during upturns. Second, labour input typically adjusts with a lag in downturns, as firms seek to retain workers even if not needed for current production so as to keep the human capital. Third, adjustment costs prevent an immediate up- or downsizing of production and capital, resulting in lower utilisation of existing capital stock in downturns. Fourth, the reallocation of resources to production of goods and services with higher or lower marginal productivities may be pro or counter cyclical.

Comparability

The appropriate measure of capital input for productivity analysis and within the growth accounting framework is the productive capital stock and its derived capital services (Annex C). While these take into account the productivity of the different capital assets, no account is taken of the extent to which the existing capital stock is actually used, i.e. the rate of capital utilisation, which may affect comparability over time and space.

Theoretically, measuring labour input by the total actual hours worked of persons employed should capture the rate of labour utilisation and hence account for the cyclical effects of labour input. Continuous labour force surveys provide a basis for measuring this. However in practice, total hours worked are often measured based on hours typically worked, or actual hours worked during a reference week which are then extrapolated over the year using additional data sources. These may not capture sufficiently variations in actual hours worked over the cycle (Annex B).

Sources and further reading

OECD Productivity Statistics (database), *http://dx.doi.org/10.1787/pdtvy-data-en*.

OECD (2009), *Measuring Capital – OECD Manual 2009: Second edition*, OECD Publishing, Paris, *http://dx.doi.org/10.1787/9789264068476-en*.

OECD (2001), *Measuring Productivity – OECD Manual: Measurement of Aggregate and Industry-level Productivity Growth*, OECD Publishing, Paris, *http://dx.doi.org/10.1787/9789264194519-en*.

Wölfl, A. and D. Hajkova (2007), "Measuring Multifactor Productivity Growth", *OECD Science, Technology and Industry Working Papers*, No. 2007/05, OECD Publishing, Paris, *http://dx.doi.org/10.1787/246367010342*.

* Official data for Germany after unification are available only from 1991 onwards. In order to estimate data for the whole of Germany back to 1985, the secretariat has estimated data for the whole of Germany back to 1970 by linking in 1991 the data for Germany to historical data for West Germany.

Figure 4.9. **Contributions to GDP growth over time**

Total economy, percentage point contributions at annual rate, G7 countries

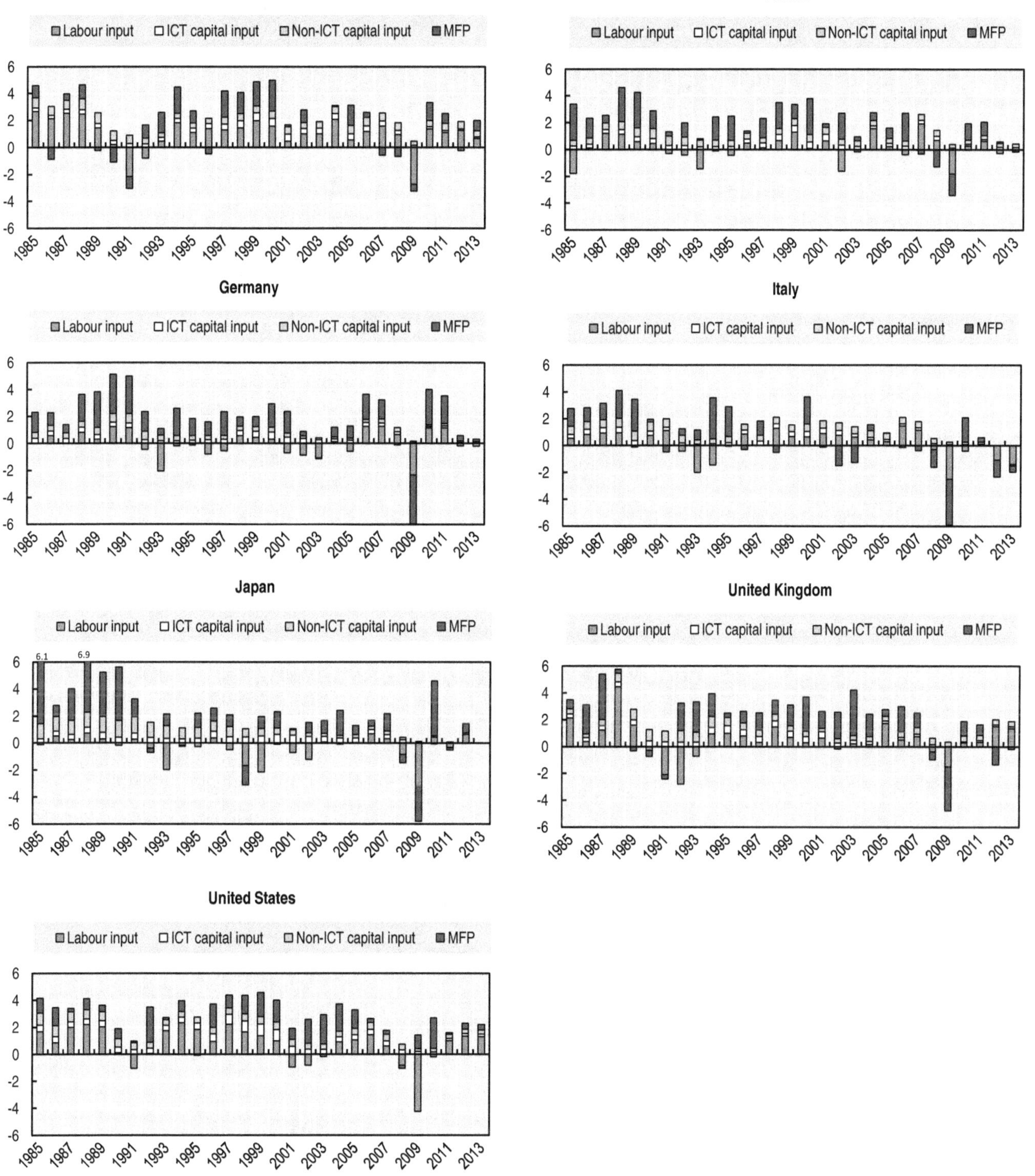

StatLink http://dx.doi.org/10.1787/888933203673

ANNEX A

Productivity measures

The *OECD Productivity Statistics* (database) (PDB) contains a consistent set of productivity measures at the total economy and at the industry levels. This annex provides detailed information on the measures included in the database.

Productivity measures for the total economy

Labour input

Within the PDB, labour input (L) is defined as total hours worked of all persons engaged in production (i.e. employees plus self-employed). The preferred source for total hours worked is the *OECD National Accounts Statistics* (database). However, this database does not provide data on hours worked for all countries, and, so, other sources are necessarily used, i.e. the *OECD Employment and Labour Market Statistics* (database). Estimates of average hours actually worked per year per person employed are also provided within the PDB. Annex B presents detailed information on hours worked.

Capital input

Capital input (K) is measured as the volume of capital services, which is the appropriate measure for capital input within the growth accounting framework (see Schreyer et al., 2003 for more details on the computation of capital services). In the PDB, capital services measures are based on productive capital stocks derived using the perpetual inventory method (PIM). The PIM calculations are carried out by the OECD, using an assumption of common service lives for given assets for all countries, and by correcting for differences in the national deflators used for information and communication technology (ICT) assets. The investment series by type of asset are sourced from national statistical offices.

From 2015, the classification of assets adopted in the PDB is in line with the 2008 SNA. Capital services are computed separately for eight non-residential fixed assets $k = 1,2,\ldots,8$, i.e. computer hardware, telecommunications equipment, transport equipment, other machinery and equipment and weapons systems, non-residential construction, computer software and databases, research and development and other intellectual property products. The volume index of total capital services is computed by aggregating the volume change of capital services of all individual assets using a Törnqvist index that applies asset specific user cost shares as weights:

$$ln\left(\frac{K^t}{K^{t-1}}\right)=\sum_{k=1}^{8}\frac{1}{2}\left(v_k^t+v_k^{t-1}\right)ln\left(\frac{K_k^t}{K_k^{t-1}}\right)$$

where:

$$v_k^t=\left(\frac{u_k^t K_k^t}{\sum_{k=1}^{8} u_k^t K_k^t}\right)$$

and u_k^t is the user cost per unit of capital services provided by asset k at time t (see Schreyer et.al., 2003). Thereby, v_k^t is the user cost share of asset k, $\frac{1}{2}\left(v_k^t + v_k^{t-1}\right)\ln\left(\frac{K_k^t}{K_k^{t-1}}\right)$ is the contribution of asset k to total capital services in year t and K_k^t is the quantity of capital services provided by asset k in year t.

Aggregate volume indices of capital services are also computed for ICT assets (computer hardware, telecommunications equipment and computer software and databases) and non-ICT assets (transport equipment, other machinery and equipment and weapons systems, non-residential construction, research and development and other intellectual property products), using the appropriate user costs shares as weights. The aggregate volume indices of ICT and non-ICT capital services are given by:

$$\ln\left(\frac{K_{ict}^t}{K_{ict}^{t-1}}\right) = \sum_{i=1}^{3}\frac{1}{2}\left(\gamma_i^t + \gamma_i^{t-1}\right)\ln\left(\frac{K_i^t}{K_i^{t-1}}\right)$$

where i represents an ICT asset and,

$$\gamma_i^t = \left(\frac{u_i^t K_i^t}{\sum_{i=1}^{3} u_i^t K_i^t}\right)$$

$$\ln\left(\frac{K_{nict}^t}{K_{nict}^{t-1}}\right) = \sum_{j=1}^{5}\frac{1}{2}\left(\gamma_j^t + \gamma_j^{t-1}\right)\ln\left(\frac{K_j^t}{K_j^{t-1}}\right)$$

where j represents a non-ICT asset and,

$$\gamma_j^t = \left(\frac{u_j^t K_j^t}{\sum_{j=1}^{5} u_j^t K_j^t}\right)$$

Cost shares of inputs

The total cost of inputs is the sum of the labour input cost and the total cost of capital services. The national accounts record the income of the self-employed *as mixed income*. This includes the compensation of both labour and capital. As such, in the PDB total labour input costs for the self-employed and employees are computed as the average remuneration per employee multiplied by the total number of persons employed. The preferred source for data on compensation of employees and for the number of employees as well as the number of self-employed is the *OECD National Accounts Statistics* (database). Whenever these data are not available in the *OECD National Accounts Statistics* (database), other sources are used, i.e. the *OECD Employment and Labour Market Statistics* (database) and national statistical authorities.

The labour input cost is calculated as follows:

$$w^t L^t = \left(\frac{COMP^t}{EE^t}\right)E^t$$

where $w^t L^t$ reflects the total remuneration for labour input in period t, $COMP^t$ is the total compensation of employees in period t, EE^t is the number of employees in period t, and E^t the total number of employed persons, i.e. employees plus self-employed, in period t.

Total capital input cost is computed as the sum of the user costs of each capital asset type k given by $u_k^t K_k^t$, where u_k^t is the user cost per unit of capital services provided by asset type k.

The total cost of inputs is then given by:

$$C^t = w^t L^t + \sum_{k=1}^{8} u_k^t K_k^t$$

and the corresponding cost shares of labour and capital are:

$s_L^t \equiv \frac{w^t L^t}{C^t}$ for labour input,

$s_K^t \equiv \frac{\sum_{k=1}^{8} u_k^t K_k^t}{C^t}$ for total capital input,

$s_{K_{ict}}^t \equiv \frac{\sum_{i=1}^{3} u_i^t K_i^t}{C^t}$ for capital input derived from ICT assets i =1,2,3,

$s_{K_{nict}}^t \equiv \frac{\sum_{j=1}^{5} u_j^t K_j^t}{C^t}$ for capital input derived from non-ICT assets $j = 1,...,5$.

Labour productivity

At the total economy level, labour productivity is measured as Gross domestic product (GDP) at market prices and at constant prices, per hour worked.

Multifactor productivity

In simple terms, growth in multifactor productivity (MFP) can be described as the change in output that cannot be explained by changes in the quantity of capital and labour inputs used to generate output. In the PDB it is measured by deducting the growth of labour and capital inputs from output growth as follows:

$$ln\left(\frac{MFP^t}{MFP^{t-1}}\right) = ln\left(\frac{Q^t}{Q^{t-1}}\right) - ln\left(\frac{X^t}{X^{t-1}}\right)$$

where Q is output measured as GDP at market prices and at constant prices. X relates to total inputs used and the rate of change of these inputs is calculated as a weighted average of the rate of change of labour and capital inputs, with the respective cost shares as weights. Aggregation of these inputs is by way of the Törnqvist index:

$$ln\left(\frac{X^t}{X^{t-1}}\right) = \frac{1}{2}\left(s_L^t + s_L^{t-1}\right) ln\left(\frac{L^t}{L^{t-1}}\right) + \frac{1}{2}\left(s_K^t + s_K^{t-1}\right) ln\left(\frac{K^t}{K^{t-1}}\right)$$

Contributions to output growth

In the growth accounting framework, growth in total output (Q) can be decomposed into the contributions to growth of each production factor plus multifactor productivity:

$$ln\left(\frac{Q^t}{Q^{t-1}}\right) = \frac{1}{2}\left(s_L^t + s_L^{t-1}\right) ln\left(\frac{L^t}{L^{t-1}}\right) + \frac{1}{2}\left(s_{K_{ict}}^t + s_{K_{ict}}^{t-1}\right) ln\left(\frac{K_{ict}^t}{K_{ict}^{t-1}}\right) + \frac{1}{2}\left(s_{K_{nict}}^t + s_{K_{nict}}^{t-1}\right) ln\left(\frac{K_{nict}^t}{K_{nict}^{t-1}}\right) + ln\left(\frac{MFP^t}{MFP^{t-1}}\right)$$

where:

$\frac{1}{2}\left(s_L^t + s_L^{t-1}\right) ln\left(\frac{L^t}{L^{t-1}}\right)$ is the contribution of labour input to output growth,

$\frac{1}{2}\left(s_{K_{ict}}^t + s_{K_{ict}}^{t-1}\right) ln\left(\frac{K_{ict}^t}{K_{ict}^{t-1}}\right)$ is the contribution of ICT capital input to output growth,

$\frac{1}{2}\left(s_{K_{nict}}^t + s_{K_{nict}}^{t-1}\right) ln\left(\frac{K_{nict}^t}{K_{nict}^{t-1}}\right)$ is the contribution of non-ICT capital input to output growth.

Contributions to labour productivity growth

By reformulating the decomposition of output growth presented above, it is possible to decompose labour productivity growth into the contribution of capital deepening and MFP.

$$ln\left(\frac{LP^t}{LP^{t-1}}\right) = \frac{1}{2}\left(s_K^t + s_K^{t-1}\right)\left[ln\left(\frac{K^t}{K^{t-1}}\right) - ln\left(\frac{L^t}{L^{t-1}}\right)\right] + ln\left(\frac{MFP^t}{MFP^{t-1}}\right)$$

where:

$ln\left(\frac{LP^t}{LP^{t-1}}\right) = ln\left(\frac{Q^t}{Q^{t-1}}\right) - ln\left(\frac{L^t}{L^{t-1}}\right)$ is labour productivity growth,

$ln\left(\frac{K^t}{K^{t-1}}\right) - ln\left(\frac{L^t}{L^{t-1}}\right)$ is capital deepening (i.e. growth in capital services per hour worked),

$\frac{1}{2}\left(s_K^t + s_K^{t-1}\right)\left[ln\left(\frac{K^t}{K^{t-1}}\right) - ln\left(\frac{L^t}{L^{t-1}}\right)\right]$ is the contribution of capital deepening to labour productivity growth.

It is also possible to reformulate the decomposition of labour productivity growth to show the contributions of ICT capital and non-ICT capital:

$$ln\left(\frac{LP^t}{LP^{t-1}}\right) = \frac{1}{2}\left(s_{K_{ict}}^t + s_{K_{ict}}^{t-1}\right)\left[ln\left(\frac{K_{ict}^t}{K_{ict}^{t-1}}\right) - ln\left(\frac{L^t}{L^{t-1}}\right)\right] + \frac{1}{2}\left(s_{K_{nict}}^t + s_{K_{nict}}^{t-1}\right)\left[ln\left(\frac{K_{nict}^t}{K_{nict}^{t-1}}\right) - ln\left(\frac{L^t}{L^{t-1}}\right)\right] + ln\left(\frac{MFP^t}{MFP^{t-1}}\right)$$

where:

$\frac{1}{2}\left(s_{K_{ict}}^t + s_{K_{ict}}^{t-1}\right)\left[ln\left(\frac{K_{ict}^t}{K_{ict}^{t-1}}\right) - ln\left(\frac{L^t}{L^{t-1}}\right)\right]$ is the contribution of ICT capital to labour productivity growth,

$\frac{1}{2}\left(s_{K_{nict}}^t + s_{K_{nict}}^{t-1}\right)\left[ln\left(\frac{K_{nict}^t}{K_{nict}^{t-1}}\right) - ln\left(\frac{L^t}{L^{t-1}}\right)\right]$ is the contribution of non-ICT capital to labour productivity growth.

Unit labour costs and their components

Unit labour costs (ULC) measure the average cost of labour per unit of output produced. They are calculated as the ratio of total labour costs to real output. At the total economy level, real output is measured as GDP at market prices and constant prices. Equivalently, ULCs may be expressed as the ratio of total labour costs per hour worked to GDP per hour worked, i.e. labour productivity.

In principle, the appropriate numerator for ULC calculations is total labour costs of all persons engaged. In practice, however, this information is not readily available for most countries. As such, OECD total labour cost estimates used in calculating ULCs are based on adjusted estimates of compensation of employees, compiled according to the *System of National Accounts* (SNA).

Compensation of employees as defined in the SNA excludes labour compensation for the self-employed which is covered in the item *mixed income*. However, the output of the self-employed contributes to value added, and, so, the OECD estimates of total labour costs include explicit adjustments to capture the labour compensation component of mixed income. This adjustment is made by multiplying compensation of employees by the ratio of hours worked for total employment to hours worked of employees.

The adjustment for the self-employed assumes that labour compensation per hour or per person is equivalent for the self-employed and employees of businesses. This assumption may be more or less valid across different countries.

Productivity measures at industry level

The conceptual approach used to estimate productivity at industry level follows that for the total economy. However the same quantity (and quality) of data that is available for the whole economy estimates is not always available at the detailed industry level. Hence some approximations are necessary and, so, some differences may prevail between the whole economy estimates and those at industry level.

Productivity measures at industry level are computed for 14 industries (activities), each defined in accordance with the International Standard Industry Classification (ISIC) Rev. 4.

Labour input

Labour input is measured as total hours worked by all persons engaged in production, i.e. employees plus self-employed, broken down by industry.

Labour productivity

At the industry level, labour productivity is measured as gross value added at basic prices and constant prices per hour worked.

Contributions to labour productivity growth

The contribution of an economic activity to labour productivity growth of a group of economic activities (e.g. total business sector, total services) is compiled as follows using a Törnqvist index:

$$Cont(i,t) = \frac{1}{2}\left[\left(\frac{Q_{cur,i,t}}{Q_{cur,tot,t}} + \frac{Q_{cur,i,t-1}}{Q_{cur,tot,t-1}}\right)\theta_t\left(Q_{con,i}\right) - \left(\frac{L_{i,t}}{L_{tot,t}} + \frac{L_{i,t-1}}{L_{tot,t-1}}\right)\theta_t\left(L_i\right)\right]$$

where:

i is an economic activity,

tot is an aggregate of economic activities including economic activity i,

Q_{cur} is gross value added at current prices,

Q_{con} is gross value added at constant prices,

L is the number of hours worked,

$\theta_t(x)$ is the annual growth rate of x between time t-1 and t.

Unit labour costs and their components

Unit labour costs (ULC) measure the average cost of labour per unit of output produced. They are calculated as the ratio of total labour costs to real output. For main economic activities, real output is measured as gross value added at basic prices and constant prices. Equivalently, ULCs may be expressed as the ratio of total labour costs per hour worked to gross value added per hour worked, i.e. labour productivity.

Total labour costs used for the calculations of ULCs by economic activity are computed as described above for the total economy.

References

OECD (2009), *Measuring Capital – OECD Manual 2009: Second edition*, OECD Publishing, Paris, *http://dx.doi.org/10.1787/9789264068476-en.*

OECD (2001), *Measuring Productivity – OECD Manual: Measurement of Aggregate and Industry-level Productivity Growth*, OECD Publishing, Paris, *http://dx.doi.org/10.1787/9789264194519-en.*

Schreyer, P. (2004), "Capital Stocks, Capital Services and Multi-Factor Productivity Measures", *OECD Economic Studies*, Vol. 2003/2, OECD Publishing, Paris, *http://dx.doi.org/10.1787/eco_studies-v2003-art11-en.*

Schreyer, P., P. Bignon and J. Dupont (2003), "OECD Capital Services Estimates: Methodology and a First Set of Results", *OECD Statistics Working Papers*, No. 2003/06, OECD Publishing, Paris, *http://dx.doi.org/10.1787/658687860232.*

ANNEX B

Measuring hours worked

Hours worked for productivity analysis – main definitions

Within the *OECD Productivity Statistics* (database) (PDB), the underlying concept for labour input is *total hours actually worked by all persons engaged in production*. It is instructive to consider the relationship between this concept and related measures of working time (Table B.1):

- *Hours actually worked* – hours actually spent on productive activities.
- *Hours usually worked* – the typical hours worked during a short reference period such as a week over a longer observation period.
- *Hours paid for* – the hours worked for which remuneration is paid.
- *Contractual hours of work* – the hours time that individuals are expected to work based on work contracts.
- *Overtime hours of work* – the hours actually worked in excess of contractual hours.
- *Absence from work hours* – the hours that persons are expected to work but do not work.

Table B.1. **Relationship between different concepts of hours worked**

Overtime hours of work					Absences from work			
Irregular overtime		Regular overtime			Irregular absence		Regular absence	
Unpaid	*Paid*	*Paid*	*Unpaid*		*Unpaid*	*Paid*	*Paid*	*Unpaid*
				Contractual hours				
				Hours actually worked				
				Hours usually worked				
				Hours paid for				

Note: Establishing the relationship between normal hours and the five other concepts is not possible, as normal hours are established on a case-by-case basis.
Source: ILO (2008), *Measurement of working time*, 18th ICLS.

Because productivity analysis is interested in measuring the inputs used in producing a given output, the underlying concept for labour input should include all hours used in production, whether paid or not. They should exclude those hours not used in production, even if some compensation is received for those hours. As such the relevant concept for measuring labour input is *hours actually worked*. The productive or non-productive characteristic of an activity is determined by its inclusion in, or exclusion from, the SNA production boundary. *Hours actually worked* are defined as (ILO, 2008):

- The hours spent directly on productive activities or in activities in relation to them (maintenance time, cleaning time, training time, waiting time, time spent on call duty, travelling time between work locations).
- The time spent in between these hours when the person continues to be available for work (for reasons that are either inherent to the job or due to temporary interruptions).
- Short resting time.

Conversely, *hours actually worked* should exclude:

- Annual leave and public holidays.
- Longer breaks from work (e.g. meal breaks).
- Commuting time (when no productive activity is performed).
- Educational activities other than on-the-job training time.

Measuring hours worked

In general, *Labour Force Surveys* (LFS) are the main source used to compile hours worked data in a majority of countries. LFS is most often also the principal underlying source in *National Accounts* – the main source ultimately used in the *OECD Productivity Statistics* (database). LFS include questions on the number of hours actually and usually worked in the reference period, and questions concerning the differences between the time usually spent working and the time actually worked during the reference week. Additional LFS questions concerning working time components such as work at home, commuting time, short breaks, overtime and absence from work are also often available.

Continuous labour force surveys are especially appropriate for measuring working time as they allow direct collection of data on hours actually worked through the year. This method is known as the *direct method*, as it is based on a direct measure of average actual hours of work during each reference week. Since the survey refers to all weeks of the year, it takes into account all types of absences from work and overtime.

However, in most cases, LFS surveys are not continuous and so the *direct method* to measure actual hours worked during the year is not applicable. In these cases, estimates are built using the *component method*. Thereby, data are collected for a specific reference week (e.g. one week during a month) and complemented with other data to build annual estimates of actual hours worked during the year. The component method starts with the usual hours of work collected in the LFS and then adjusts for absences from work such as holidays, bank holidays, illness, maternity leave, overtime, etc. Annual totals are then derived by scaling up the weekly estimate.

In some countries, LFS surveys are not used or are complemented with information from other sources. Among such other sources are the following:

- *Establishment (and enterprise) surveys*. These are typically the main source of information for hours worked estimates by industry. One of the main drawbacks of this source is that the data collected generally refer to hours *paid* rather than actual hours *worked*, hence include paid absences and exclude unpaid overtime.

- *Administrative records,* such as social security and tax registers. These are the main sources of information for adjusting data from labour force surveys and establishment surveys to obtain estimates of absences from work due to illness, maternity leave, occupational injuries, strikes and lockouts.
- *Time Use Surveys.* These are useful to compare the results from other sources but their irregularity, low frequency and limited international comparability is a drawback. Labour force survey based estimates of working time typically over-report hours worked when compared to estimates from time use surveys.

For productivity analysis, consistency of LFS based data on hours worked with the *National Accounts* concepts needs to be ensured (OECD, 2009; Ypma and van Ark, 2006). This implies adjusting the coverage of activities included in the LFS to that used to compute GDP, and adapting the geographical and economic boundaries of employment to GDP. The notion of economic territory used to compute GDP refers to the domestic concept, i.e. resident persons working outside the country are excluded. Some of these adjustments can be considered as negligible for most countries although they are made in all countries. Likewise, measures of hours actually worked should refer to productive activities within the SNA production boundaries (by definition); persons spending time on productive activities excluded from the original sources should therefore be included.

In general, when LFS is the main source of information for employment, adjustments concern persons outside the LFS universe but who need to be included as persons engaged in production, as defined in the SNA. The causes for differences between these two measures are:

- Age threshold (e.g. people under 15 engaged in production are generally not included in LFS estimates).
- Non-coverage of particular groups: persons living in collective households, armed forces, and non-resident persons working within the economic territory of the country are generally not surveyed in LFSs.
- Non-coverage of certain activities: The LFS may not include hours worked in certain activities such as subsistence work and volunteer work.
- Non-coverage of some territories: The LFS may not cover the entire economic territory covered in GDP.

Hours worked data in the *OECD Productivity Statistics* (database)

In the *OECD Productivity Statistics* (database), the main requirement is that the most internationally comparable hours worked data are used (OECD, 2007). The default source for total hours worked is generally the *National Accounts* which are presented in the *OECD National Accounts Statistics* (database), both for the total economy and for aggregate economic activities. However, long time series of hours worked are not available for a number of countries; in which case, the Secretariat estimates hours worked using the *OECD Employment and Labour Market Statistics* (database), which is based on annual national LFS results supplemented with information from a detailed OECD survey sent to member countries. Total economy estimates of average hours actually worked per year and per person employed are currently available on an annual basis, for all 34 OECD member countries as follows:

- Actual hours worked are primarily sourced from the *OECD National Accounts Statistics* (database) for Australia, Austria, Belgium, Canada, the Czech Republic, Denmark, Estonia, Finland, France, Germany, Greece, Hungary, Ireland, Israel, Italy, Korea, Luxembourg, Mexico, the Netherlands, Norway, Poland, Portugal, the Slovak Republic, Slovenia, Spain, Sweden, Switzerland, the United Kingdom and the United States.
- Actual hours worked are sourced from the *OECD Employment and Labour Market Statistics* (database) for Chile, Iceland, Japan, New Zealand and Turkey.

References

ILO (2008), *Measurement of working time*, 18th ICLS.

OECD (2009), "Comparability of labour input measures for productivity analysis", *Document prepared for the OECD Working Party on National Accounts*, November, *www.oecd.org/officialdocuments/publicdisplaydocumentpdf/?doclanguage=en&cote=std/cstat/wpna(2009)11*.

OECD (2007), "Factors explaining differences in hours worked across OECD countries", *Document prepared for the Working Party No. 1 on Macroeconomic and Structural Policy Analysis*, September.

Ypma, G. and B. van Ark (2006), "Employment and Hours Worked in National Accounts: A Producer's View on Methods and a User's View on Applicability", *EU KLEMS Working Paper*, No. 10.

ANNEX C

Capital input measures at the OECD

Introduction

Two key measures of capital stock exist. The first is *productive capital stock*, which looks at capital in its function as a provider of capital services in production. The second is gross (or net) capital stock, which captures the role of capital as a store of wealth.[1] This annex provides supplementary information on these two measures, the approaches used to estimate them and capital measures available at the OECD.

Definition

Productive capital stock (and capital services)

When the purpose of capital measurement is to gauge its role in production and productivity, via capital services, it is necessary to construct measures of the *productive capital stock*. The productive capital stock per type of capital asset is constructed by applying an age-efficiency profile and a retirement pattern when past investments of each asset are summed up over time. For example, a 10-year old lorry would be given a lower weight compared to a new lorry when past purchases of lorries are added up to construct a measure of today's productive stock of lorries. Moreover, lorries are scrapped after a certain number of years and investments that date back by say 30 years would not enter today's productive stock. Unlike gross or net capital stock measures, aggregate productive stock measures weight different types of assets by their relative productivity using the user costs of each capital type. The resulting aggregate constitutes a measure for the potential flow of productive services that all fixed assets can deliver in production.

Net and gross (wealth) capital stocks

Perhaps the best known measure of capital stock is that used to value assets on a company, industry or nation's balance sheets, that is, the gross or net capital stock measures described in the *System of National Accounts* (SNA). These provide measures of wealth but they are not conceptually appropriate for productivity analysis. Unlike the productive stock, the purpose of wealth capital stocks measures is not to track the role of capital as a factor of production but to track the role of capital as a set of assets with market value – wealth capital stocks appear on the balance sheets in the SNA. This reflects the fact that the implicit weighting for the different assets used in building up wealth measures of capital stock is based on the market values of the different assets. However changes in the relative productivity of the different assets are not necessarily consistent with changes in the relative price of the assets. For productivity analysis it is the former measure (and weighting of different asset types) that is relevant.

Measuring capital input

In general, capital stock series are not directly measured. In common with most measures presented in the national accounts, they are estimated by national statisticians using available underlying data with local methodology and assumptions – although there is increasing convergence towards international standards. There are heavy data requirements for the estimation of capital stocks which include the following:

- A benchmark level of capital stock for at least one year (preferably by asset type).
- A long-time-series of investment volumes and price deflators (preferably by asset type).
- As much asset type detail as possible.
- Depending on the type of capital stock being estimated, estimates of average services lives by asset and/or depreciation rates for each asset.
- Industry-by-asset-type investment matrices for capital stock by industry.

In this publication, capital input measures (i.e. capital services) are in line with the 2008 SNA, with the exception of Portugal, which capital input measures are still on a 1993 SNA basis. An important recommendation of the 2008 SNA is to recognise research and development expenditure as investment. The 2008 SNA also recommends to extend the scope of fixed capital formation with the inclusion of expenditures on military equipment.

Capital measures in OECD statistics

Several OECD databases, described below, contain capital stock data. However some differences exist between them:

- *The origin of the data.* In some of the databases described below only official data made available to the OECD by national statistics institutes are used. In other databases however, particularly those that are considered more analytical databases, such as the *OECD Productivity Statistics* (database), other sources are often used to estimate missing data or to create estimates based on comparable estimation techniques.
- *The coverage of the data.* As shown in Table C.1, some databases are confined to aggregate statistics, such as the *OECD Economic Outlook* (database) or the *OECD Productivity Statistics* (database). Others provide a break-down by industry, such as the *OECD Structural Analysis Statistics* (database) and the *OECD National Accounts Statistics* (database).
- *The capital stock variable.* The *OECD Productivity Statistics* (database) measures productive capital stocks whereas the *OECD Structural Analysis Statistics* (database) and *OECD National Accounts Statistics* (database) contain measures of net and/or gross capital stocks.

Table C.1. **Asset and industry breakdown of capital stock data in OECD databases**

		Asset breakdown	
		Yes	No
Industry breakdown	Yes	*OECD National Accounts Statistics* (database)	*OECD Structural Analysis Statistics* (database)
	No	*OECD Productivity Statistics* (database)	*OECD Economic Outlook* (database)

Capital services for the total economy, 8-way asset break down

Estimates of capital services in the *OECD Productivity Statistics* (database) (PDB) are based on a common computation method for all countries (Schreyer et al., 2003). This approach estimates productive stock for all countries on the assumption that the same service lives are applicable for any given asset irrespective of the country.[2] The approach further uses harmonised deflators for computer hardware, telecommunications equipment and computer software and databases, for all countries, to sort out comparability problems that exist in national practices for deflation for this group of assets.

From 2015, the classification of assets adopted in the PDB is in line with the 2008 SNA asset boundary. The flows of capital services are computed separately for eight non-residential fixed assets: computer hardware, telecommunications equipment, transport equipment, other machinery and equipment and weapons systems, non-residential construction, computer software and databases, research and development and other intellectual property products. By their very nature, capital services flows are presented as rates of change or indices and not as levels of stocks as is the case for measures of net and gross stocks.

Net and gross capital stocks by broad economic activities, with 9-way asset break-down

The *OECD National Accounts Statistics* (database) brings together a large number of national accounts series for OECD and non-OECD countries. This includes data on net and gross capital stocks broken down by main economic activity and by nine types of assets (dwellings, other buildings and structures, transport equipment, other machinery and equipment and weapons systems, of which computer hardware and telecommunications equipment; cultivated biological resources; intellectual property products, of which computer software and databases and research and development. The data are transmitted by OECD member countries in reply to an official questionnaire and are provided in current prices and volumes. The level of industry detail and the time period covered varies across countries.

Net and gross capital stocks by detailed industries, no asset break-down

The *OECD Structural Analysis Statistics* (database) (STAN) provides data on volume measures of *gross and net capital stock* by industry. STAN is currently moving to a new ISIC Rev. 4 based industry list which covers all ISIC Rev. 4 aggregations used for national accounts, some additional 2- and 3- digit ISIC Rev. 4 detail, as well as specific aggregates. The level of industry detail and the time period covered varies across countries. A detailed overview of available data in STAN can be found at *www.oecd.org/sti/stan*.

Alternative capital stocks, for the total economy, no asset break-down

The *OECD Economic Outlook* is a key twice-yearly publication with economic forecasts and analyses for OECD countries. One of the series available is the volume measure for non-residential capital services for the total economy (productive capital stocks).

How to access OECD capital input measures

- Aggregate capital services series in PDB, along with methodological information and analytical papers and publications can be found on the OECD Productivity Statistics website on *www.oecd.org/std/productivity-stats/* or on the PDB on OECD.Stat, within the theme *Productivity*, then selecting *Growth in GDP per capita, productivity and ULC*, and then *Growth in capital input*.
- Data on gross/net capital stocks by industry can be found in the STAN database on: *www.oecd.org/sti/stan*.
- Gross/net capital stocks in the *OECD National Accounts Statistics* (database) can be found under the theme of the national accounts via: *http://stats.oecd.org/*, then selecting *Annual National Accounts*; *Main Aggregates*; *Detailed Tables and Simplified Accounts*; *Fixed Assets by Activity and by Type of Product*.
- Data used for the *OECD Economic Outlook*, such as the total economy productive capital stock volume series, are published separately and can be found under the item *Supply Block* through the current *OECD Economic Outlook* theme on OECD.Stat (*http://stats.oecd.org/*).

Notes

1. For more information on capital measures and their uses see OECD (2001, 2009a, 2009b) and Schreyer (2004).
2. The following average service lives are assumed for the different assets: 7 years for computer hardware, 15 years for telecommunications equipment, other machinery and equipment and weapons systems and transport equipment, 40 years for non-residential construction, 3 years for computer software and database, 10 years for research and development and 7 years for other intellectual property products.

References

OECD (2009a), *Handbook on Deriving Capital Measures of Intellectual Property Products*, OECD Publishing, Paris, *http://dx.doi.org/10.1787/9789264079205-en.*

OECD (2009b), *Measuring Capital – OECD Manual 2009: Second edition*, OECD Publishing, Paris, *http://dx.doi.org/10.1787/9789264068476-en.*

OECD (2001), *Measuring Productivity – OECD Manual: Measurement of Aggregate and Industry-level Productivity Growth*, OECD Publishing, Paris, *http://dx.doi.org/10.1787/9789264194519-en.*

Schreyer, P. (2004), "Capital Stocks, Capital Services and Multi-Factor Productivity Measures", *OECD Economic Studies*, Vol. 2003/2, OECD Publishing, Paris, *http://dx.doi.org/10.1787/eco_studies-v2003-art11-en.*

Schreyer, P. (2002), "Computer Prices Indices and International Growth and Productivity Comparisons", *Review of Income and Wealth*, No. 1, Series 48.

Schreyer, P., P. Bignon and J. Dupont (2003), "OECD Capital Services Estimates: Methodology and a First Set of Results", *OECD Statistics Working Papers*, No. 2003/06, OECD Publishing, Paris, *http://dx.doi.org/10.1787/658687860232.*

SNA (2008), *System of National Accounts 2008*, New York, *http://unstats.un.org/unsd/nationalaccount/sna2008.asp.*

SNA (1993), *System of National Accounts 1993*, New York, *http://unstats.un.org/unsd/nationalaccount/sna1993.asp.*

ANNEX D

The System of National Accounts 2008

The 2008 SNA – changes from the 1993 SNA

In 2009, the United Nations Statistical Commission endorsed a revised set of international standards for the compilation of national accounts: the *System of National Accounts* (SNA) 2008, replacing the 1993 version of the SNA. The indicators presented in this publication are based on the 2008 SNA for all OECD countries except Chile, Japan, Norway and Turkey. For Portugal, growth accounts are presented on a 1993 SNA basis whereas the labour productivity and unit labour cost indicators are presented on a 2008 SNA basis. For New Zealand, growth accounts are presented on a 2008 SNA basis whereas the labour productivity and unit labour cost indicators are presented on a 1993 SNA basis. The 2008 SNA includes a number of changes from the 1993 SNA and was adopted by most OECD countries at the end of 2014.

Changes affecting whole economy levels of income

For the United States, the adoption of the 2008 SNA in 2013 raised the level of GDP by 3.6%, mainly due to the recognition of new forms of gross fixed capital formation (GFCF), notably Research and Development (R&D). The revision was also an opportunity for countries to implement some additional changes made in the 1993 SNA, which recognised entertainment originals as fixed assets. In addition changes were also made for the 2008 SNA recommendations on ownership transfer costs (see below). Current consumption expenditures of government in recent years were also revised downwards, reflecting 2008 SNA recommendations on defined benefit pensions plans as well as the net (of depreciation) effects of removing R&D expenditures from current consumption (see also below).

Research and experimental development

Research and Development (R&D) is recognised for the first time as a produced asset. This also means that payments for the acquisition of patents, treated as acquisition or disposal of non-produced, non-financial assets in the 1993 SNA, are treated as transactions in produced assets. This also has implications for sectoral gross value added as the 2008 SNA also recommends that a separate establishment be distinguished for R&D producers when possible. See also the OECD Handbook on Deriving Capital Measures of Intellectual Property Products. Under the 1993 SNA, expenditure on R&D by government already adds to government output (which is estimated on a sum of costs basis) and subsequently as general government final consumption. So, for government the direct impact of the capitalisation mainly involves a reclassification of expenditure from government final consumption to government gross fixed capital formation (GFCF). Indirectly however government output and, so GDP, will increase as part of the costs of government is an imputation for depreciation; which now includes a component for the capital stock of R&D by government.

Weapons systems

Military weapons systems such as vehicles, warships, etc. used continuously in the production of defence (and deterrence) services are recognised as fixed assets in the 2008 SNA (the 1993 SNA recorded these as fixed assets only if they had dual civilian use and as intermediate consumption otherwise). Some single-use items such as certain types of ballistic missiles with a highly destructive capability, but which provide ongoing deterrence services, are also recognised as fixed assets in the 2008 SNA. Because most if not all of these expenditures are carried out by government (whose output is typically valued by summing costs) GDP will only increase by the related new consumption of fixed capital.

Financial Intermediation Services Indirectly Measured (FISIM)

The method recommended in the 2008 SNA for the calculation of FISIM implies several changes from that in the 1993 SNA. For example it explicitly recommends that FISIM only apply to loans and deposits provided by/deposited with financial institutions, and that for financial intermediaries all loans and deposits are included, not just those of intermediated funds. In addition, the 2008 SNA no longer allows countries to record FISIM as a notional industry.

Financial services

The 2008 SNA defines financial services more explicitly to ensure that services such as financial risk management and liquidity transformation, are captured.

Output of central banks

The 2008 SNA has provided further clarification on the calculation of FISIM in calculating the output of centrals banks. Where Central Banks lend or borrow at rates above or below the effective market lending/borrowing rate, the 2008 SNA recommends the recording of a tax or subsidy from the counterpart lender/borrower to/from government to reflect the difference between the two rates. Correspondingly a current transfer (the counterpart to the tax/subsidy) is recorded between government and the Central Bank. These flows will have an impact on the distribution of income in national income compared to the 1993 SNA treatment.

Output of non-life insurance services

The methodology used to indirectly estimate this activity in the 1993 SNA (premiums plus premium supplements minus claims) could lead to extremely volatile (and negative) series in cases of catastrophic losses. The 2008 SNA recommends a different indirect approach to measurement that better reflects the pricing structures used by insurance companies and the underlying provision of insurance services *per se*. The approach can be simply described as an *ex ante* expectation approach. Output is equal to premiums plus expected premium supplements minus expected claims. The 2008 SNA also recommends that exceptionally large claims, following a catastrophe, be recorded as capital, rather than current, transfers which will have an impact on (particularly sectoral) estimates of disposable income.

Valuation of output for own final use

The 2008 SNA recommends that estimates of output for own final use should include a component for the return to capital as part of the sum of costs approach when comparable market prices are not available. However no return to capital should be included for non-market producers.

Costs of ownership transfer

The 1993 SNA recommended that these costs (treated as GFCF in the accounts) should be written off over the life of the related asset. The 2008 SNA instead recommends that these costs be written off over the period the asset is expected to be held by the purchaser. This will impact on measures of net income and only marginally on gross measures, reflecting the calculation of output for own final use and government output (which is calculated as the sum of costs including depreciation).

Re-allocating income across categories

Goods sent abroad for processing

The 2008 SNA recommends that imports and exports be recorded on a strict ownership basis. This means that the values of a flow of goods moving from one country (that retains ownership of the goods) to another providing processing services should not be recorded. Only the charge for the processing service should be recorded in the trade statistics. The 1993 SNA imputed an effective change of ownership.

Merchanting

Under the 1993 SNA merchanting – the purchase and subsequent resale of goods abroad without substantial transformation and without the goods entering or exiting the territory of the merchant – was classified as a services transaction. This treatment caused global imbalances in goods and services because while the merchant records an export of a service the country acquiring the good records an import of a good. Therefore, the 2008 SNA recommends classifying merchanting as a component of trade in goods. The acquisition of goods by the merchant are recorded as negative exports of the merchant's economy and the subsequent resale of goods by the merchant are recorded as a positive exports. The difference between sales and purchases of merchanted goods is recorded under a new category "Net exports of goods under merchanting" of the merchant's economy.

Defined benefit pension schemes

The 1993 SNA stated that actual social contributions by employers and employees should reflect the amounts actually paid. The 2008 SNA differs, recognising that the amounts actually set aside may not match the liability to the employees. As such, the 2008 SNA recommends that the employer's contribution should reflect the increase in the net present value of the pension entitlement plus costs charged by the pension fund minus the employee's own contributions. This change will result in a shift of income between gross operating surplus and compensation of employees and between institutional sectors (corporations/government and households).

In some cases, a defined benefit pension plan may be underfunded implying the pension plan has insufficient financial assets to earn the returns that are necessary to meet promised future benefits. The promised future benefits are assets of the household sector and liabilities of the pension schemes, or the employer if there is no autonomous scheme. According to the 1993 SNA, only the funded component of pension plans should be reflected in liabilities. However, the new 2008 SNA recognises the importance of the liabilities of employers' pension schemes, regardless of whether they are funded or unfunded. For pensions provided by government to their employees, countries have some flexibility in the recording of the unfunded liabilities in the set of core tables. However, the full range of information is required in a new standard table (SNA Table 17.10) that shows the liabilities and associated flows of all private and public pension schemes, whether funded or unfunded, including social security.

Ancillary activities

The 2008 SNA recommends that if the activity of a unit undertaking purely ancillary activities is statistically observable (separate accounts, separate location) it should be recognised as a separate establishment.

Holding companies

The 2008 SNA recommends that holding companies should always be allocated to the financial corporations sector even if all their subsidiary corporations are non-financial corporations. The 1993 SNA recommended that they be assigned to the institutional sector in which the main group of subsidiaries was concentrated.

Exceptional payments from public corporations

The 2008 SNA recommends that these should be recorded as withdrawals from equity when made from accumulated reserves or sales of assets. The 1993 SNA treated such transactions as dividends.

Exceptional payments from governments to quasi-public corporations

The 2008 SNA recommends that these should be treated as capital transfers to cover accumulated losses and as additions to equity when a valid expectation of a return in the form of property income exists. The 1993 SNA treated all such payments as additions to equity.

References

SNA (2008), *System of National Accounts 2008*, New York, *http://unstats.un.org/unsd/nationalaccount/sna2008.asp*.

SNA (1993), *System of National Accounts 1993*, New York, *http://unstats.un.org/unsd/nationalaccount/sna1993.asp*.

van de Ven, P. (2015), "New standards for compiling national accounts: What's the impact on GDP and other macro-economic indicators?", *OECD Statistics Brief*, No. 20, OECD Publishing, Paris, *www.oecd.org/std/na/new-standards-for-compiling-national-accounts-SNA2008-OECDSB20.pdf*.

ANNEX E

Measuring producer prices and productivity growth in services

The price index-productivity link

Empirical evidence presented in this publication points to relatively low productivity growth rates over long periods for several service industries. This is true even for some business sector services for which rapid technological change and increasing competitive pressures may argue for an opposite trend. However, for some services, this evidence may reflect an under-estimation of service productivity growth, linked to difficulties measuring price indices, and hence volume series of services value added (Wölfl, 2003). While problems estimating an appropriate price index may arise in several manufacturing industries, there are reasons that measurement problems may be stronger in the service sector than in manufacturing.

Because of the difficulty in measuring services producer price indices (SPPIs), different methods are used in OECD countries to compute volume series of value added. Moreover, even if producer price indices can be computed, different methods are typically used depending on the type of the service under consideration as well as data and availability. Over the past ten years, much progress has been made by OECD countries in measuring SPPIs, in particular in business sector services. This has significantly increased the availability of SPPIs and has improved their comparability across countries. However, even where SPPIs have been computed, they are based on different pricing methods across industries and countries, potentially affecting comparability of productivity growth estimates.

General measurement issues when tracking price changes for services

Measurement of price changes in services is not trivial, in large part complicated by the way businesses provide and charge for services, by problems identifying quality change, through the provision of bundled services, and by the difficulty identifying separate price indices per end-user.

Pricing methods

The way businesses provide and charge for services can make it difficult for statisticians to observe prices for a repeated service transaction. As such, standard price measurement methods designed for repeated products can be difficult to apply for services. In practice, price statisticians are then obliged to use a number of methods to track price changes in services, with the methods typically varying across countries, depending on the pricing mechanisms used, and also on the producing industry or product.

However, over the last ten years, considerable efforts have been made by price statisticians to provide a better understanding of the variety of methods used by countries to facilitate international comparability and hence improve matters. The three main classes of pricing methods[1] are:

- **Price of final service output:** Price observations refer directly to specified service outputs and result in prices of final services output; examples are: direct use of prices of repeated services, contract pricing, unit value, percentage fee, component pricing and model pricing.
- **Time-based prices:** Price observations refer to the time used for the provision of the service rather than to the service itself. Several time-based methods can be distinguished: hourly charge out rate, hourly list rate, wage rates and working days.
- **Margin prices:** Price observations refer to the price that would have to be paid by the service provider for the good or service they provided and the price paid by the final consumer.

It is important to bear in mind that how firms in a given sector charge for their products can impact considerably on the reliability of measured prices indices of the index for the industry. For example, when price indices are either based on a specified service output or are time-based, results of pricing methods can have a different interpretation. In the first case, the volume of output is, in principle, correctly measured (albeit depending on how well price-determining factors are specified). However, this is not necessarily the case for time-based methods, particularly whenever quality changes have occurred, or productivity changes impact on the input (hours spent). Indeed, for pricing based on working time, the price of the service finally provided is not identified. Rather, service provision is assumed to correspond directly or predominantly to different types of chargeable hours, actually worked for a client. The validity of the method depends on how realistic this assumption is, i.e. to what extent the quantity and quality of one chargeable hour's work remains the same in consecutive periods.

Quality changes

While in principle, the same quality adjustment methods can be used for goods and services, in practice, for services, fewer options are available and much more difficult to implement (Loranger, 2012). First, over time, the way in which a certain service is provided may change (e.g. a service is delivered in less time or by a better qualified employee). Second, the structure of services that are provided in a certain service industry will vary from one period to the next. Third, many service products are unique. In this case, prices cannot be observed over multiple periods requiring assumptions about quality changes that are mostly based on convention rather than reflecting "reality"; typically, constant quality is assumed.

Treatment of bundled services

Services are frequently (and increasingly) bundled with either another service or a good. This is particularly true in the case of Transport and storage and Information and communication services. Two main alternatives are commonly used: i) breaking down the bundle into components and price these separately; or ii) pricing bundled services together as a group. Each of these alternatives poses difficulties that are likely to imply biased measure of prices. A particular concern is keeping the bundle constant over time either through quality adjustment or regular updating of the selected bundled services. The ability to reflect the non-monetary benefits of the bundle in the price index may also be a complicated task. Finally, the treatment of bundled services may lead to a heavy calculation and response burden, in particular where bundled components are priced separately.

Decomposition by type of end-users

Breaking down SPPIs by type of user is an important requirement for the national accounts when price discrimination occurs which feeds through into heterogeneous price changes. Currently, decompositions of SPPI by type of end-users focus mainly on Business to Business (BtoB), Business to Consumers (BtoC) and Business to All (BtoAll) transactions.

The potential role of price measurement for measured productivity growth

Table E.1 provides some indication of the potential effects on volume series of value added that may result from using different deflators for two services "Telecommunication services", on the one hand, and "legal and accounting services", on the other.[2] These services provide two interesting examples of how price index measurement could impact on measured productivity growth.[3] They are: i) characterised by very different factors of service output and the way they are provided; and ii) by different availability of producer price indices and underlying methods.

Table E.1. **Average annual growth rates in gross value added per person employed using different deflators of value added, in %**

			Base	Wage rate employment	CPI – all items	CPI – related service	SPPI
France	Telecommunications services	2000-10	6.37	0.55	2.71	6.32	
		2005-10	4.73	-2.01	0.22	4.92	8.60
	Legal and accounting services	2000-10	-0.24		1.17	1.02	
		2005-10	-1.18	-3.26	-0.88	-1.58	-2.70
United States	Broadcasting and telecommunication	2000-10	6.82	2.28	1.88	7.41	6.00
		2005-10	5.64	0.40	0.85	5.67	3.12
	Legal services	2000-10	-1.60	-0.28	0.53	-1.65	-2.68
		2005-10	-3.00	-1.13	-0.36	-1.88	-4.12

Note: All results based on double deflation. "Base": value added deflator as given in National Accounts.
Source: OECD, *OECD Structural Analysis Statistics* (database); INSEE, Bureau of Labour Statistics.

The table provides evidence for France and the United States, for which time series data are available for a large range of input and output variables, such that several different price and volume indices can be derived. The different deflators compared are those that are commonly used in countries either directly for a deflator of value added or as a reference for the computation of producer price indices:

- *Producer Price Indices (SPPI).* From a methodological point of view, using SPPIs, especially in the form of a *price of final service output* as defined above, would represent the most appropriate way to deflate value added if the aim is the computation of productivity growth. Ideally, SPPIs would exist for both, gross output and intermediate inputs used in producing the good or service under consideration, and SPPIs would adjust for quality changes so that the resulting value added volume series reflect productivity growth changes properly.
- *Consumer Price Indices (CPI),* for goods or services that are close to the services analysed, or the *CPI All items.* Using CPI's for deflation may result in measurement biases *vis-à-vis* SPPIs as they cover only household consumption and are not valued in basic prices. This may be particularly relevant for those services where the share of final household consumption in total output is low, and where price changes differ significantly between intermediate (business) and final use (consumption) (Eurostat, 2001).
- *Wage rate indices* per employed person or per hour worked (WRIE, WRIH). The latter can be seen as a proxy for a *time-based producer price index* as defined above. Productivity growth rates based on wage rate indices may underestimate true productivity developments.

The table suggests that the choice of the implicit value added deflator, or the pricing method for computing producer price indices, may matter significantly for measured labour productivity growth. For instance, in telecommunication services, average annual labour productivity growth rates over the 2000-11 period would differ by between 5 percentage points (the United States, both periods) and 10 percentage points (France, 2005-11) using different deflators. In the case of legal services, the overall variation is with 1 to 4 percentage points lower, but still significant, especially given the generally lower level of productivity growth in this services activity.

Notes

1. A pricing method is a procedure put in place by statisticians to make price data eligible to be entered in an index which is largely determined by the *pricing mechanism* (Fraisse, 2013).
2. This exercise is of a purely hypothetical nature. Its aim is to simulate how value added volume series and hence productivity growth could be affected if different pricing methods were used.
3. In the empirical results presented in Table E.1, labour productivity growth has been calculated as real value added per employment and not per hour worked. While hours worked is typically the more appropriate measure of labour input, employment has been chosen here for data availability reasons.

References

Eurostat (2001), *Handbook on price and volume measures in national accounts*, Eurostat, Luxembourg.

Fraisse, A.S. (2013), "The New SPPI Guide, Issues and Challenges", *Paper presented for the Ottawa Group Meeting*, Statistics Denmark, Copenhagen, 1 May, OECD, Paris, *www.dst.dk/da/Sites/ottawa-group/~/media/Kontorer/12-Priser-og-forbrug/Ottawa-Group/Anne-Sophie%20Fraisse%20ASF_SPPI_OttawaGroup.pdf.*

Loranger, A. (2012), "Quality Change for Services Producer Price Indexes", *Paper presented at the Group of Experts on Consumer Price Indices*, Geneva, Switzerland, 30 May-1 June.

Wölfl, A. (2003), "Productivity Growth in Services Industries: An Assessment of Recent Patterns and the Role of Measurement", *OECD Science, Technology and Industry Working Papers*, No. 2003/07, OECD Publishing, Paris, *http://dx.doi.org/10.1787/086461104618.*

ANNEX F

Trends

Understanding to which extent productivity growth is driven by structural factors and affected by short-term economic fluctuations is of utmost importance for policy makers. To shed light on this distinction, one can decompose the series into a trend and a cyclical component, where the trend is meant to capture the long-term growth of the series and the cyclical component is the deviation of the series from that trend. In the *OECD Compendium of Productivity Indicators 2015*, the method used to extract the trend component is the Hodrick-Prescott (HP) filter (Hodrick and Prescott, 1997).

The Hodrick-Prescott filter

The HP filter is the best known and most widely used method to separate the trend from the cycle (Hodrick and Prescott, 1997). The method has been first presented in a working paper in 1981 (Hodrick and Prescott, 1981). The filter is defined as the solution to the following optimisation problem:

$$y_t = \tau_t + c_t$$

$$min_{\{\tau_t\}} \left\{ \sum_{t=1}^{T} (y_t - \tau_t)^2 + \lambda \sum_{t=2}^{T-1} \left[(\tau_{t+1} - \tau_t) - (\tau_t - \tau_{t-1}) \right]^2 \right\}$$

where y_t is the original series, τ_t is the trend component and c_t is the cyclical component. The method consists of minimising the deviation of the original series from the trend (the first term of the equation) as well as the curvature of the estimated trend (the second term). The trade-off between the two goals is governed by the smoothing parameter λ. The higher the value of λ, the smoother is the estimated trend.

For quarterly data it has been typically assumed a value of λ = 1 600, as recommended by Hodrick and Prescott (1997). However, there is less agreement on the value to be used when the filter is applied to other frequencies (e.g. annual, monthly). Backus and Kehoe (1992) used λ = 100 for annual data, while Ravn and Uhlig (2002) propose an adjustment of the standard value of 1 600 that consists of multiplying that value by the fourth power of the frequency of observations relative to quarterly data. The latter results in a value of λ equal to 6.25 (1 600*(1/4)^4) for annual data.*

The HP-filter can be interpreted in the frequency domain. In this formulation the λ parameter can be associated with the cut-off frequency of the filter – the frequency at which it halves the impact of the original cyclical component. It can be shown that the Ravn-Uhlig rule for selecting the value of λ corresponds to a cut-off frequency of approximately 10 years, assuming annual data (Maravall and Del Río, 2001). Nonetheless, Nilsson and Gyomai (2011) point out that the HP-filter has strong leakages (i.e. letting cyclical components from the stop band appear in the filtered series), and this feature may affect the choice of the filter parameter depending on the goal of the study and sensitivity to filter leakage.

* The frequency of observations relative to quarterly data is 1/4 for annual data and of 3 for monthly data.

In this publication, the target frequencies for trend estimation was no different than in the above studies (10 years and beyond). However an additional objective is to minimise the leakage from shorter business-cycle frequencies into the estimated trend. Accordingly, the value of the smoothing parameter selected here is $\lambda = 54.12$. This value has been determined by calibrating the Hodrick-Prescott filter in such a way that the frequency response at 9.5 years is equal to 0.10. This means that with $\lambda = 54.12$, cycles with a wavelength lower than 9.5 years would be attenuated by 90% or more.

To analyse the impact of the λ parameter, the HP trend has been calculated using alternative values for the smoothing parameter ($\lambda = 6.25$ and $\lambda = 100$). The trends estimated with the different values of λ are available in this file *www.oecd.org/std/productivity-stats/OECD-Compendium-of-Productivity-Indicators-2015-Annex-F.xlsx*.

In comparison with other *ideal* filters, the trend estimated with the HP filter is more sensitive to transitory shocks or short-term fluctuations at the end of the sample period. This results in a sub-optimal performance of the HP filter at the endpoints of the series (Baxter and King, 1999). In view of this property, in order to lessen revisions of the published estimates, trend series are not published for the last two years for which data on the original series are available. Even though, the choice of the HP filter is based on its interpretability and widespread use in the literature.

References

Backus, D.K. and P.J. Kehoe (1992), "International evidence on the historical properties of business cycles", *The American Economic Review*, Vol. 82, No. 4.

Hodrick, R.J. and E.C. Prescott (1997), "Postwar US Business Cycles: An Empirical Investigation", *Journal of Money, Credit and Banking*, Vol. 29, No. 1.

Hodrick, R.J. and E.C. Prescott (1981), "Postwar US Business Cycles: An Empirical Investigation", *Discussion Paper*, No. 451, Carnegie Mellon University.

Maravall, A. and A. Del Río (2001), "Time aggregation and the Hodrick-Prescott filter", *Documento de trabajo*, No. 0108, Banco de España, Servicios de Estudios.

Nilsson, R. and G. Gyomai (2011), "Cycle Extraction: A Comparison of the Phase-Average Trend Method, the Hodrick-Prescott and Christiano-Fitzgerald Filters", *OECD Statistics Working Papers*, No. 2011/04, OECD Publishing, Paris, *http://dx.doi.org/10.1787/5kg9srt7f8g0-en*.

Ravn, M. and H. Uhlig (2002), "On adjusting the Hodrick-Prescott filter for the frequency of observations", *The Review of Economics and Statistics*, Vol. 84, No. 2.

ORGANISATION FOR ECONOMIC CO-OPERATION AND DEVELOPMENT

The OECD is a unique forum where governments work together to address the economic, social and environmental challenges of globalisation. The OECD is also at the forefront of efforts to understand and to help governments respond to new developments and concerns, such as corporate governance, the information economy and the challenges of an ageing population. The Organisation provides a setting where governments can compare policy experiences, seek answers to common problems, identify good practice and work to co-ordinate domestic and international policies.

The OECD member countries are: Australia, Austria, Belgium, Canada, Chile, the Czech Republic, Denmark, Estonia, Finland, France, Germany, Greece, Hungary, Iceland, Ireland, Israel, Italy, Japan, Korea, Luxembourg, Mexico, the Netherlands, New Zealand, Norway, Poland, Portugal, the Slovak Republic, Slovenia, Spain, Sweden, Switzerland, Turkey, the United Kingdom and the United States. The European Commission takes part in the work of the OECD.

OECD Publishing disseminates widely the results of the Organisation's statistics gathering and research on economic, social and environmental issues, as well as the conventions, guidelines and standards agreed by its members.

OECD PUBLISHING, 2, rue André-Pascal, 75775 PARIS CEDEX 16
(30 2015 01 1 P) ISBN 978-92-64-22953-2 – 2015

www.ingramcontent.com/pod-product-compliance
Lightning Source LLC
LaVergne TN
LVHW081418110826
845149LV00010B/1793

* 9 7 8 9 2 6 4 2 2 9 5 3 2 *